"Truth is so obscure in these tim___ ___
that, unless we love the t___ ___

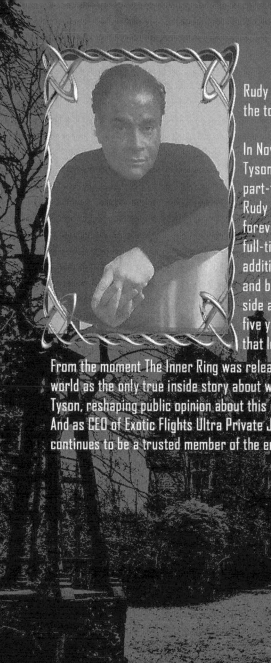

Rudy Gonzalez was born and raised in the tough streets of Spanish Harlem.

In November of 1986, he met Mike Tyson by chance on his first job as a part-time limousine driver. Little did Rudy know his life would change forever when Tyson hired him as his full-time chauffeur, later giving him additional duties as his personal aide and bodyguard. Rudy was at Tyson's side around the clock for more than five years, the only person to survive that long in Tyson's "Inner Ring."

From the moment The Inner Ring was released, it has rocked the boxing world as the only true inside story about what really happened to Mike Tyson, reshaping public opinion about this greatest heavyweight of all time. And as CEO of Exotic Flights Ultra Private Jet Service, Rudy Gonzalez continues to be a trusted member of the entertainment world to this day.

THE INNER RING

The Set-Up of Mike Tyson and
The Uncrowning of Don King

Surfside Six Publishing

ISBN 978-0-692-04632-6

Library of Congress Control Number: 2017915927

Printed in the United States of America

Surfside Six Publishing
P.O. Box 545960
Surfside, Florida 33154
Tel: (305) 868-1223 Fax: (844) 274-0862
Rudy Gonzalez - Rudy@TheInneRing.com
Martin A. Feigenbaum - miamivicelaw@aol.com

In Memory of Gus D'Amato
For giving Mike Tyson the tools he needed to
become the greatest heavyweight champion of all
time and for being the father he never had.

FOREWORD

The Inner Ring first appeared on the publishing scene in May of 1995, about one month after Mike Tyson was released from a Plainfield, Indiana prison. He had spent more than three years there for his conviction in the rape of Desiree Washington, a beauty-pageant contestant. The book immediately ignited a firestorm of controversy. On May 17, 1995, Michael Katz wrote in the *New York Daily News* that Tyson's chauffeur maintained his boss went to prison because "Don King was afraid to lose him to another promoter." Katz said *The Inner Ring* "was a better buy than the pay-per-view on Tyson's first fight back."

On May 18, 1995, boxing columnist Jon Saraceno wrote about *The Inner Ring* in *USA Today*, the article entitled "Book Portrays Tyson As Puppet of King." Not long after that, *USA Today* published another Saraceno piece, "Team Tyson: Ring Dynasty Or King-Size Cult?" In the *Las Vegas Sun*, sports writer Dean Juipe had an article about *The Inner Ring*, "Tyson's Bodyguard Lowers Boom On King." Juipe stated: "It's a scathing book with a ring of truth to it, especially since the targets aren't talking about litigation. As Don King's publicist said: 'He's not even bothering with it,' as if the only hope of lessening the impact of Rudy Gonzalez's accusations is to ignore them."

Rudy Gonzalez was raised in the tough streets of New York's Spanish Harlem. In the very early morning of November 29, 1986, while on his first job as a limousine driver, Rudy met Mike Tyson. Rudy's life soon would change forever when "Iron Mike" asked him to become his full-time chauffeur, later adding the responsibilities of personal aide and bodyguard. Rudy worked for Tyson for more than five years, the only person to survive that long in his "inner ring." But that wild ride ended in early 1992 when an Indianapolis jury found Mike Tyson guilty of the rape of Desiree Washington.

I met Rudy in early 1995. He wanted to tell this story so that the world would know what *really* happened to Mike Tyson. Rudy insisted we finish *The Inner Ring* before Tyson was released from prison. Although we didn't meet that goal, we came pretty close. Of course, there would be those who doubted parts of Rudy's story. But it wasn't long before those doubters became true believers. Years later, in 2013, Mike Tyson published his autobiography, *Undisputed Truth*, which corroborated Rudy's account about what had befallen the greatest and, without a doubt, most controversial fighter of all time. One thing is certain: *only* Rudy, the humble servant by his side for so many years, could relate with such gripping detail what *really* had happened to Mike Tyson.

In May and June of 1995, when *The Inner Ring* ran its first and second printings, Amazon had not yet made its debut as an online bookseller. And it wasn't until 2007 that Amazon introduced the Kindle, its first e-reader. Now, in this digital age, *The Inner Ring* is available from online bookstores and downloads for e-readers like the Kindle. A timeless saga, *The Inner Ring* has returned because, as Don King was so fond of saying: *"You've gotta understand..."*

Martin Alan Feigenbaum
Surfside, Florida
December, 2017

"This is a book that only could have been written by someone who loved Mike Tyson and was his devoted man Friday as well as his personal chauffeur.

Rudy Gonzalez was not only at Mike's service and present at all times, as it turned out he was more! He was the "fly on the wall" so to speak.

Here Rudy reveals some of the most sad and shocking stories behind the headlines and behind the facades. An incredible story told by Rudy Gonzalez with the superb collaboration of Martin Feigenbaum."

Bill Cayton

June 6, 1918 – October 4, 2003
Bill Cayton, Tyson co-manager from the original "Team Tyson"

Dedication

To Alfonso "Grandpa" Miranda, "Let's get to the point." You made it all happen.

To My Beloved Father, Big Rudy, for keeping the world off my shoulders. There isn't a night when I don't think of you. Rest in peace forever.

To My Beautiful Mother, Elizabeth, thank you for giving me life, hope, and dreams, and for being my strength every day.

To My Little Sister, Evelyn, no matter what the world does, I will hold your hand and walk with you until the end of time.

To Marty Feigenbaum, for being a heavyweight champion of words and for never giving up on me or Tyson. For helping me write a modern-day tragedy which I lived for so many years.

To Bobby Paulino, for knocking out the visual story for me and for your dedication to the project for more than ten years.

Denise with her husband Roger, daughter Erica and son Roger Jr.

"I am sorry that I failed, that I could not protect Mike Tyson against Don King and his evil empire. The Inner Ring is dedicated to you, that it may stand forever as a record of what happened to your brother. What nobody really understands is the night you passed away, Mike died inside. From that moment on, he was filled with great despair and agony which never would heal because he had lost the only one he truly loved. You would be so proud of your children. Roger Jr. is a kind and caring man, Erica Monique is a beautiful and caring mother and Roger Sr. continues to be a caring and loving father. You continue to live through them. Denise, I will never forget you."

Rudy Gonzalez

"Yo"

"The Jacket"

"Gotta Have it, Givens"

"Bait & Switch"

"The Kingdom of Darkness"

"From the Darkness Comes a Whisper"

"Just Sign Here"

"Final Errands"

"The Final Round"

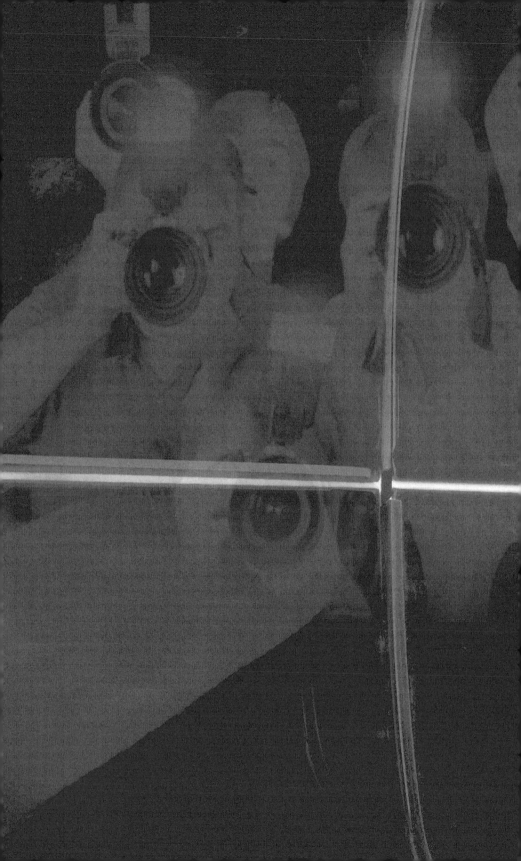

"YO!"

The first year I drove Mike Tyson around he acted like he didn't know my name. He just called me "Yo!" Before that amazing new chapter in my life began, I was working full-time during the day for United Parcel Service. I also had been hired as a part-time night driver for Michelle's limousine service. Around 3:00 a.m. on a very cold day in late November of 1986, someone placed a credit-card order to pick up an unknown party at Kennedy Airport. The dispatcher called me because the job was too much of a dog for one of the regular drivers. Although I had been on Michelle's list of part-timers for more than three months, this was going to be my first job. A few days before, on November 22, 1986, Mike Tyson had captivated the world by winning the WBC heavyweight title, knocking out Trevor Berbick in the second round at the Las Vegas Hilton. At age twenty, that victory made "Iron Mike" the youngest heavyweight champion in history. Had the dispatcher known the party waiting at JFK was the famous newly-crowned world champion, she never would have assigned me that job.

In early 1992, a jury found Mike Tyson guilty of raping Desiree Washington, an eighteen-year-old Miss Black America beauty contestant. By that time, more than anyone else, I knew what *really* had been going on in Tyson's life. By that time, I had heard and seen too much, having been with

Tyson around the clock for nearly five years. By that time, I was the most dangerous man in the boxing world, even though I wasn't a professional fighter, because I had learned the truth about what had befallen Mike Tyson. A few days after we discovered the extent of the fraud and deception, sitting on the floor of Tyson's bedroom in Las Vegas, I was the victim of an assassination attempt while running an errand in Los Angeles.

Mike Tyson disappeared behind the walls of an Indiana prison wearing inmate number 922335. How could it be that one of the most famous athletes of all time, worth hundreds of millions of dollars, and with countless beautiful women pursuing him, would end up in a cold prison cell for rape? This book answers that question. *The Inner Ring* is the only truly eye-opening account about what *really* happened to "Iron Mike" Tyson from someone who survived longer than anyone else in his most "inner ring."

***

By pure coincidence I happened to be watching an episode of *Entertainment Tonight* when Playboy Enterprises announced it was taking a new direction. To get "in tune with the eighties," Playboy decided it also should develop a female clientele. Consequently, it decided that Playboy Clubs would have "rabbits" as well as "bunnies." The next morning I was on the phone getting information about the "rabbit" auditions. Three days later I went to Playboy Enterprises with a photo and a bathing suit. After sizing up the competition, I was convinced that I didn't stand a chance. After standing in line for hours, my turn finally came. Parading around in only my swimming trunks, I felt very foolish. Almost everybody was being sent away with a simple "thank you." Somehow I had made it to the final level and was hired as a "rabbit" who fit the "Hispanic profile." Stationed at the Octagon Bar, I was taking home $300 to $500 a night, a huge extra income for me at age twenty-four. During the two years I worked at the Playboy Club, I noticed it attracted a strange mix, like Elizabeth Taylor, Dr. Ruth Westheimer, Sylvester Stallone, Malcolm Forbes, Howard Stern, Montel Williams, and Gregory Hines. On one occasion Mike Tyson showed up with a group of people, including LL Cool Jay and Run-D.M.C., but I didn't meet my future boss that night.

My time at the Playboy Club provided me with money and sex far beyond my wildest dreams. There were women waiting around every night to see if they could take home a "rabbit." And the gorgeous "bunnies" preferred to hook up with "rabbits" because we were trusted fellow employees. It was a total fantasy existence while it lasted. One day Playboy Enterprises announced it was closing its entire chain of Clubs. I was surprised because it seemed like a very profitable business. However, the world was changing fast, and the Playboy Club's image no longer was "politically correct." The company flew all of us out to Los Angeles, put us up in a nice hotel for several days, and invited us to the Playboy Mansion for a big farewell bash. After that trip, my wild and profitable days as "Rudy The Rabbit" were over.

One of the guys from my neighborhood was Hector Camacho who became boxing great "Macho" Camacho. As a young kid, Hector took a lot of crap from his *compadres* for being a "pretty boy." He started boxing to develop a reputation as a "bad ass." Anybody who teased him about his good looks would end up getting his ass kicked. Years later incredible circumstances would make our paths cross again in the world of professional boxing, and there would be both intrigue and betrayal.

Pleasant Avenue was the unofficial border between the Italian and Puerto Rican neighborhoods. I could hang out in either one with impunity because I had blood and friends on both sides. I had a very bad streak in me and had shown it to a lot of people. But I got along well with just about anybody unless they violated my trust. It was probably because I was this way that I survived longer than anyone else at Mike Tyson's side as he rose to acquire enormous fame, fortune, and power.

***

I was at a point now in my life where I was getting desperate to find some excitement. With all the stories I had heard, I became obsessed with becoming a limo driver. Ruth Goldberg, whom I had met while serving drinks at the Playboy Club, owned a limousine company called Michelle's which had a celebrity clientele. Her customers liked the fact she had a fleet of Rolls Royces. I went by her place of business, and she greeted me warmly. She said her company could use me and had me fill out an application. But three months went by without a single call while I kept working my day job at United Parcel Service.

Around 3:00 a.m. on November 29, 1986 the phone rang. My mother, Elizabeth, answered the call, then yelled out some lady was asking for me. Before she handed me the phone, she wanted to know what the hell I was doing taking a job with a limo service where I would be out all night and lose my job at UPS. I told her that I was looking for some excitement, not to worry, that I could do both.

"Gonzalez, this is the dispatcher. Your name is on our standby-drivers list. Get your butt down to the garage. We've got a pick-up at JFK."

The winter of 1986 was very harsh. There was a lot of snow on the ground, and the cold air blasted me in the face as I tried to flag down a private cab. You couldn't find a Yellow Cab at that hour in Spanish Harlem no matter what time of year. I was getting nervous because I had to get to 125th and Riverside Drive in the next few minutes, or I would be fired for sure without ever having driven my first limo. Finally, a gypsy cab slowed down, and I could see the driver checking me out. Dressed in a black suit, white shirt, and trenchcoat, I must have looked decent enough so I was on my way to Michelle's. When the driver pulled up to the garage and honked, a heavy metal door slowly rose, revealing three sparkling Rolls Royce Silver Spurs, two regular length and one double. I was very anxious to get behind the wheel. I had been waiting for this moment for three months.

"Take whichever one you want," the dispatcher told me. "Your pick-up is at Kennedy. It's a prepaid credit-card job. The passenger will recognize the limo when you get there. You'll get instructions from the client."

The hourly charge was $85, one-hour minimum, and I would get 20% of the total fare plus a 5% gratuity. I jumped in the double-length Silver Spur and started trying to figure out all the gadgets. It was an impossible task in a short time so I pulled out and headed toward JFK which was about twenty minutes away. From the moment I was on the road, sitting behind this gorgeous, luxurious piece of machinery, I knew that I was going to love this job.

The dispatcher told me that my passenger would be

waiting for the limo at the international terminal. It was deserted outside so I parked and called the dispatcher who told me to look around inside the building. If the client couldn't be located, the company still would pay me for one hour. I didn't see anybody who looked like they were expecting a Rolls Royce limousine so I started to head back outside. Just as I was exiting the terminal I noticed a black man sleeping in a fetal position, his body half-resting on a window ledge, head covered by the hood of his jacket. He appeared to be a homeless person seeking refuge from the bitter cold. But something was wrong with that picture because a very expensive-looking leather bag was lying on the floor next to him.

"Excuse me, sir. Did you order a limo?"

The man raised his head and pulled open the hood. I couldn't believe it. Staring back at me was Mike Tyson, the newly-crowned heavyweight champion of the world.

"Yeah, man, I called for you. Where's the limo?" He put his hood back on and stood up. "Grab that," he said, gesturing at the Louis Vuitton bag next to him.

I was very nervous because Mike Tyson was going to be my first passenger. I was sure that I was going to mess up and never have the chance to drive a limo again. Millions of people around the world had been following Tyson's incredible career during the past two years. Professional boxing is a passion where I come from, and Tyson was a fighter who grew up nearby in the Brownsville section of Brooklyn. With his heavyweight championship victory over Trevor Berbick just the week before, anybody who read the newspaper or watched television recognized Mike Tyson. But I never realized just how massively built he was until I personally witnessed up close his bulging twenty-inch-plus neck and tree-trunk legs.

Mike Tyson instructed me to take him to Bentley's, a nightclub in midtown Manhattan. He closed the glass partition separating us and talked on the phone the entire duration of the trip. When we arrived at Bentley's, he jumped out and bolted inside, leaving me in the bitter cold for more than an hour. When he emerged, Tyson was surrounded by a group of his friends, everyone laughing at some joke one of them had just told.

"Yo, check out this limo," Tyson said, ushering his friends over to the curb, showing off the double-length Silver Spur. He opened the passenger door, and they all poked their heads inside *oohing* and *aahing* their approval. Then Tyson said that he was real tired and would hook up with them tomorrow. He slid inside the limo and lowered the partition. "Hey, Yo, drive me home now!"

"Where's home, sir?"

"In the Catskills. A couple of hours north." Tyson gave me directions and told me to wake him up when we got close. "Then I'll tell you how to get to my house."

As Mike Tyson raised the glass partition, I began thinking about whether I was going to make it to work on time the next day. My mother was right. I was going to lose my job at UPS if I kept working as a limousine driver. My famous passenger didn't make a sound during the entire trip. I woke him up when we reached the town of Catskill. Tyson was rested now, was very polite, and gave me directions to his house.

For the last few miles there was nothing but woods. I made the final turn onto a narrow road which ended at the driveway of a large three-storey colonial-style house. A fourteen-passenger grey Mercedes limousine was parked there, and it was almost twice as long as my Rolls Royce "eight-pack." The driver of that limo was asleep behind the wheel. Mike Tyson jumped out, and I followed three steps behind him. He banged on the driver's window, and the old man inside appeared momentarily confused before he opened the door. The Mercedes limo had a raspberry-colored interior, the passenger compartment converted into a master bedroom with a bar and a television.

Tyson told his chauffeur that Jim Jacobs, one of his co-managers, had attempted to reach him repeatedly with no response so he had to find a limousine service in the middle of the night. The old man apologized, claiming that nobody had contacted him to let him know that his boss would be flying into Kennedy Airport.

"Get out of the car. Don't worry about not picking me up cause you're fired. Give the keys to my man here."

Tyson shrugged in my direction, then headed up to the house, the poor chauffeur following, apologizing and begging to keep his job. Tyson just waved him away.

"You drive for me now," Tyson said, turning to me. The old man knew he wasn't going to change Tyson's mind and handed me the keys to the fourteen-pack Mercedes.

I was stunned at just being awarded the position of Mike Tyson chauffeur on my first trip out as a limo driver. I had only exchanged a few words with Tyson during the past ten hours.

"Sir, I can't do that," I said without thinking. "I have a regular job at UPS. In fact," I continued, pointing at my watch, "I'm supposed to be at work in three hours. This is the first limo job I ever had."

Tyson snatched the keys from me. I asked him to sign the job ticket and confirm the total time he had used the service. He scribbled his initials, pulled something out of his pants pocket, and returned the ticket to me. There were three one-hundred dollar bills rolled up inside as a tip.

"Thank you, sir, but I can't take this." I handed the cash back to him. "It was an honor just driving for you."

"Okay," he said and continued on to the house.

I fetched the Louis Vuitton bag from the limo, handed it to Tyson, and headed back to the City, hoping to be able to report on time at UPS. Wow, was I feeling great! Everything had gone without a hitch. I didn't get lost on the trip to Catskill or wreck the limo. And I was going to make around one-hundred dollars for driving the newly-crowned heavyweight boxing champion of the world in one of the finest luxury automobiles on the planet.

When I pulled into the limo company garage, Ruth was there and asked me how the job had gone. When I told her that my passenger was Mike Tyson, she got very upset. Had she known it was going to be a celebrity, the company would have contacted one of its experienced drivers. It turned out the caller who had requested the service was not Jim Jacobs but Bill Cayton, the other Tyson co-manager whose name the dispatcher had not recognized.

Three things occurred that very cold November 29, 1986 morning which landed me the job that would forever change my life and that of Mike Tyson: Tyson's regular chauffeur could not be located, Michelle's dispatcher did not know the request for service was for a celebrity, and I was available from the standby-driver list at 3:00 a.m.

"Don't worry, everything went fine," I told Ruth, hoping my first drive for Michelle's wasn't going to be my last. "He even offered me a job as his chauffeur."

"Don't believe it, Rudy," she smiled. "Celebrities say the same thing to my drivers all the time."

***

Life returned to normal for me after the trip to Catskill. Hardly anybody at UPS believed that I really had met Mike Tyson. And, even if I had, nobody believed that Tyson had asked me to go to work for him. By the end of December I was getting more jobs as a part-timer for Michelle's which had a contract with one of the big hotels. I didn't get any more celebrities to drive around, mostly business people from other countries. The trips usually involved taking passengers to fancy restaurants, the theater, or the opera. My ten-hour drive for Mike Tyson appeared to have been a once-in-a-lifetime stroke of luck.

Just like my days at the Playboy Club, I once again was getting used to surviving on very little sleep, juggling my time between UPS and the limo service. But I was learning how to be a professional chauffeur, its special courtesies and protocols and, to a great extent, learning how to spend countless hours in the limousine waiting for clients to return from wherever I had dropped them off.

On December 31, 1986, Ruth called me and said that Mike Tyson had ordered one of her limos and insisted that I be his driver. In the early afternoon I was dispatched to Marlborough House to pick up Tyson's older sister, Denise, and some of her friends and drive them to meet up with Tyson in the Catskills. Denise was severely obese, weighing close to four-hundred pounds. On February 21, 1990, at age twenty-four, Denise died from cardiac arrest.

When we arrived a few hours later, my passengers piled out, slipping and sliding wildly on the snow-covered driveway. I remained inside the limo awaiting further instructions. By then I had learned it was not part of my job to bother a client about what I was supposed to do next. A few minutes later a very elderly white lady carefully made her way down the driveway to the Rolls Royce.

"I am Camille," she said, with a foreign accent, handing me a cup of hot chocolate and some cookies wrapped in a paper napkin. I assumed she was the live-in maid. However, before long I would learn this residence, known as "The White House," was Camille Ewald's house which she had shared for many years with Constantine "Cus" D'Amato, her life-long companion.

Cus D'Amato was one of the true boxing legends. He had managed and trained several champions, including Floyd Patterson and Jose Torres. Camille and Cus brought Tyson into their home when he was thirteen. After Tyson's mother passed away, D'Amato formally adopted him. I didn't see Mike Tyson while he was visiting inside with his sister and the others I had picked up in Manhattan. However, several hours later, he finally emerged from The White House, accompanied by a hulking, seven-foot, three-hundred-pound black man, Caesar, his bodyguard.

"Hey, Yo, take us back to the City."

I don't think Mike Tyson knew my name yet. He just kept calling me "Yo." During more than five years that I constantly was at his side, I always addressed Mike Tyson as "Sir." Eventually, Tyson insisted I call him "Mike." I said "sure" but continued to call him "Sir" except on rare occasions. When we arrived back in the City, Tyson and Caesar stopped at several clubs, including Studio 54 and Bentley's. Tyson then asked me to take them over to Jersey. They were going to "Bubble Hill," Eddie Murphy's mansion in Englewood. I couldn't believe it! Things were getting even better for me in my quest for excitement. At the time, Eddie Murphy was on top of the world, a superstar, riding a huge wave of blockbuster movies.

When we arrived at the four-acre property a little before midnight, there already were dozens of limos parked outside. It was obvious a major bash was taking place. Through the picture window I could see lots of beautiful girls running around in bikinis. Tyson left Caesar outside with me. I spent some of my time talking with the other chauffeurs and observed the comings and goings of the celebrities, mostly black musical personalities, like Al B. Sure!, Bobby Brown, Run-D.M.C., and Heavy D. Tyson sent me three times to pick up friends from his old Brownsville neighborhood. I ended up shuttling a total of six hours between Englewood and Brooklyn that night.

Around eleven the next morning, while I was in a deep sleep, Tyson tapped on the driver's window. He was surrounded by three very pretty young black girls.

"Yo, where's my movies?"

Tyson always took video cassettes wherever he went. I located them inside an expensive designer bag he had left in the back of the limo. He showed the girls the available selection, and they finally decided on one to stick in the VCR before piling into the back of the Rolls.

"Hey, Yo, take me to the Catskills," he said as the glass partition went up.

I had been on this job almost twenty-four hours, and now there would be at least another six. I didn't hear anything from my passengers until we arrived at The White House which, being my third trip there, I had no problem finding on my own. I asked Tyson to sign the job ticket with all these extra hours so I wouldn't get in trouble for keeping the limo out for so long. Again Tyson wanted to tip me, and again I refused.

"It's no problem, Sir. I'll see you next time."

He looked very confused. "Yo, you don't want no money, man? What's up with you?"

Tyson insisted that I take my time getting back to the City and ordered me to add several more hours on the ticket to make sure all my time would be covered. To my surprise, he reached out and gave me a hug around the neck. It was the beginning of a tradition which Tyson carried on until the very end to show his appreciation when I handled a job for him respectfully and professionally.

"I'll call you when I need you."

I noticed the fourteen-pack Mercedes limousine was still parked in the driveway in the exact same spot it had been that first night I had seen it back in November.

***

Almost three months went by without Mike Tyson requesting me as his driver. At The White House on New Year's Day, he had said he would call when he needed me. I figured he must have come into the City dozens of times during that period. I remembered what Ruth had told me after my first Tyson job, that celebrities are always making promises they never intend to keep. Both my jobs were slowing down after the holiday season. I only had a few calls from Michelle's for airport runs. Then the dispatcher called one day and said Tyson had requested that I pick up a white male named Jay Bright and take him around Manhattan for some sightseeing and shopping. Jay had been one of the troubled kids, like Tyson, whom Cus and Camille took in and cared for at The White House.

On March 7, 1987, at the Las Vegas Hilton, Mike Tyson won a unanimous twelve-round decision over James "Bonecrusher" Smith, adding the WBA heavyweight title to his WBC title. A few weeks after that victory, I received a message at UPS to call Ruth at Michelle's. At that time I was working 6 a.m. to 3 p.m. mostly sorting packages.

"Mike Tyson called and wants you to pick up one of the Rolls and go to Atlantic City." I could tell by her tone that Ruth was upset with this job order.

"Is there a problem?"

"The problem is we've got a system here, a seniority system. I've got drivers sitting around doing nothing with a lot more experience than you, especially for top clients. And you've got another full-time job anyway."

"If you've got a problem, then you should discuss it with Mike Tyson."

Ruth didn't respond for a few moments, then said there was a clean Rolls ready for me and hung up.

By 4:00 p.m. I was heading down the Jersey Turnpike with the Atlantic City address where Mike Tyson was staying. I told the doorman at the Ocean Club who I was. He assured me he would let Mr. Tyson know right away that I had arrived. About two hours later Mike Tyson descended from the penthouse and gave me that same hug around the neck. Then we headed out for some shopping with an entourage of Tyson's friends from his old neighborhood. He seemed very relaxed and happy that afternoon.

I had to call UPS and request time off because that one afternoon turned into three full days. When I called Michelle's to let them know how long the job was going to take, Ruth got on the line. Again she sounded upset. Ruth had a rule that drivers had to check in every hour, and I hadn't been in touch for half a day. And then she became very agitated, accusing me of "negotiating" the extended job directly with Mike Tyson when that business decision wasn't mine to make. She started rambling about splitting up twenty-four hours of work among three drivers. Ruth wasn't making any sense, and I couldn't understand why she was complaining. The prestigious client was happy with me, and this job meant non-stop income for her company during the several days it lasted. I wasn't about to burden Mike Tyson with Ruth's silly rules so I told her I had to get going and hung up.

At the end of the third day, Tyson asked me to run one of his friends back to Brooklyn and turn in the limo. He gave me the customary hug, told me to add six hours as a tip, signed the ticket, and said he'd call when he got back to the City. I figured I couldn't count on Ruth to give me any more jobs, especially if the client were Mike Tyson, so I left my beeper number with him. One afternoon in May I received a page around 2:00 p.m. and called the number. It was Tyson calling from The White House in Catskill.

"Yo, I want a limo up at my house by 8:00 p.m."

I called Ruth right away to book a Rolls for Tyson. She wanted to know why he was dealing directly with me. It was clear Ruth was putting an end to this procedure. She was tired of Tyson requesting one particular driver because that's not the way things worked at Michelle's.

I gave her the number at The White House. "You call him if you've got a problem with me taking the job," I said. She told me that's exactly what she was going to do. An hour later, Al Salvy, the manager at the UPS hub, came to see me. We weren't on very good terms by that time. I had received several promotions and now was in charge of supervising all deliveries into Brooklyn. Rivalries among the various ethnic groups, blacks, Puerto Ricans, Anglos, Orientals, was a way of life in the City, and UPS was no different. But I did everything I could to turn our cultural mix into a team. I tried to be fair and flexible and covered for the guys I supervised when they had emergencies or family problems. Everybody worked their assess off. We had a great record, zero "service failures" for three consecutive months, meaning no packages were lost or delivered late during that period. Salvy didn't like the way I got along with everybody because that wasn't normal. He was convinced that I wanted his job.

"Gonzalez, I'm sick and tired of people calling you up here at work," Salvy barked at me. "You waste a lot of company time with that chauffeur bullshit. Now there's somebody on the line impersonating Mike Tyson."

"It *is* Mike Tyson."

"Yeah, right," he said, giving me the finger as he turned and walked away.

I went to Salvy's office and pressed the button on the flashing line.

"Yo, what's up with that bitch at the limo office?"

"Sir, I don't have control over the company rules."

"I'm tired of this bullshit," Tyson said. "What are you doing now?"

"Sir, I don't get off from work for another hour. What do you want me to do?"

There was a short pause, then Tyson said: "I'll work out something else for right now. You quit your job and come work for me. Go down later to the heliport at 34th and East River Drive. There's a chopper waiting for you."

There was a sharp click as Tyson hung up. I looked around Al Salvy's office. There was a certificate on the wall showing appreciation for his twenty-five years of faithful service. I saw myself going nowhere. If I were lucky, maybe I would be standing in his shoes twenty-five years down the road, tired and bitter. Mike Tyson had said a helicopter was waiting for me so what was I waiting for? I picked up the phone and called my mother. I told her Mike Tyson had offered me a full-time job. She wasn't happy about the idea of my giving up a good job for something without a future. My father was still doing time in prison, and she wanted me to have a safe and stable life.

I strolled aimlessly around the building, realizing I never was going to be a big shot in a company like United Parcel Service. And I was pretty sure Ruth wasn't going to give me any more work so I was at the end of my exciting part-time career driving for the limo service. I found my boss sitting in the cafeteria taking his afternoon break and announced that I was quitting.

"What's your problem now, Gonzalez?"

"Mike Tyson offered me a job."

He shook his head and raised his eyes to the ceiling.

"Would you please stop the bullshit."

"I'm outta here," I said and walked away.

Al Salvy was both shocked and mad. There wasn't anybody to replace me right away. I gave my co-workers the news, and they cheered and slapped me on the back. I raced back to our tiny apartment in Spanish Harlem and packed a small bag. In the taxi on the way to the heliport, I began feeling regret and insecurity. What the hell was I doing? I had just quit a good-paying supervisor's job with a major corporation. I had no idea how much I was going to earn working for Mike Tyson or how long the job would last. It also dawned on me I was going to work for somebody who acted like he still didn't know my name, calling me "Yo" six months after I first met him in the early hours of one very cold November morning.

"The Jacket"

"THE JACKET"

Donald J. Trump recently had acquired Pan Am's helicopter service, adding it to his collection of real estate and hotel properties. The taxi pulled up to a construction trailer which served as Trump Air's mini-terminal at the heliport. Several helicopters were parked nearby bearing the logos of local tv stations. I entered the trailer and told the lady behind the counter that I was going to Atlantic City, that Mike Tyson was supposed to have made advance arrangements for me.

"Oh, yes, you must be Mr. Gonzalez," she said with a big smile. "Your helicopter is en route. And," she added, reaching underneath the counter and then handing me a large white box, "Mr. Tyson left something for you."

Within a few moments there was a tremendous roar which violently shook the trailer.

"Mr. Gonzalez, there you go," the woman shouted, pointing toward the door.

Setting down very delicately was an enormous black Huey helicopter marked "TRUMP." A hostess saw me and beckoned me inside. When the doors closed, the deafening roar suddenly was replaced by total silence.

"Please fasten your seatbelt, Mr. Gonzalez."

We lifted off, swinging out at a forty-five-degree angle, heading west over Manhattan toward the Hudson River. I was the only passenger. The chopper was fitted with elegant wrap-around couches, and huge gold "T's" were displayed throughout its interior. This had to be Donald Trump's personal helicopter.

The hostess asked me if I would like something to eat and drink so I ordered a Coke and some peanuts. I asked myself again: "What the hell am I doing here?" But for the moment there wasn't much I could do at 8,000 feet, the enormous power of the Huey hurtling us toward Atlantic City. I sat back and sunk into the plush dark-chocolate leather. The hostess called Atlantic City and began making arrangements for our arrival. I decided to open the large white box Tyson had left for me at the Trump Air counter. Inside there was a red-white-and-blue leather fight jacket. "World Heavyweight Champion" it said on the back and had Tyson's image stitched in various shades of leather. Later I would learn this jacket had been crafted by Jeff Hamilton, the celebrity apparel maker, and it was worth more than $5,000. I kept staring at the jacket's incredible beauty and finally turned it over. I then realized that Mike Tyson really did know my name. On the front of it, embroidered in big letters, it said "RUDY."

***

Before we landed in Atlantic City, the hostess told me I was going to have a quick sightseeing tour of the area. She pointed out some of the hotels, including those where Tyson had crushed four of twenty-eight opponents during his undefeated, meteoric rise to heavyweight champion in less than two years. There was Resorts International where Tyson knocked out Ricardo Spain and Lorenzo Canady in the first round, the Atlantis where he disposed of Robert Colay in the first round, and the Trump Plaza where he polished off John Alderson in the second, Mike Jameson in the fifth, and Jose Ribalta in the tenth round. Then the hostess pointed toward a beautiful thirty-storey luxury condominium building. It was the Ocean Club where Mike Tyson resided in its penthouse.

As the helicopter touched down, I could see in the distance a huge hole where construction was underway for the next Trump hotel, the Taj Mahal. As the door dropped down, I was greeted by four big black guys, including Tyson's bodyguard, Caesar. A small crowd was waiting nearby, expecting to be able to catch a glimpse of "The Donald." Instead they got the poor Puerto Rican kid from Spanish Harlem. Caesar grabbed my hand and shook it warmly, then introduced me to Jaymore, Ouie, and Bill.

As we made our way toward his car, Caesar tapped me on the shoulder. "You're part of the team now."

Caesar presented me to the doorman and some of the other personnel at the Ocean Club, informing them I was a member of the Tyson crew. Things were moving too fast. I was very curious why Mike Tyson had placed such great confidence in me so quickly.

Later I would learn that Tyson had seen in me something different. I always had been very respectful and business-like, keeping my distance even after so many hours driving him around. On that first trip in November, when I picked him up at Kennedy Airport and took him to Bentley's, ending up ten hours later at The White House in Catskill, I had refused a $300 tip. I told him that it was an honor just driving him around. The next time I drove for him, I also refused a big tip. Mike Tyson came to understand I wasn't interested in taking his money. After he became wealthy and famous, there had been very few people like me in his life.

"Let's go up," Caesar said after taking me around. "MT's waiting to see you."

We got into a key-access-only express elevator that whisked us up to the penthouse floor. The living room had a glass ceiling which gave it the effect of a crystal palace. Everything was done in white, rugs, furniture, huge marble sculptures, and there were pillows stitched in gold. Portraits of the fighter hung on the walls. It was very quiet inside, servants coming and going without making a sound.

In the middle of the living room, Mike Tyson sat back on a beautiful white leather sofa, dressed only in lycra athletic shorts. A diamond Rolex dangled from his wrist. His ruby-and-diamond-clustered WBC Championship ring reflected sunlight pouring through the glass roof. Tyson was speaking in a low voice on a portable phone. He waved me in and gestured for me to take a seat.

Before that day I had met people with money while driving for Ruth's limousine service. I had seen the inside of fine hotels, apartment buildings, and restaurants and been to the Playboy Mansion. But that day, after my ride in Donald Trump's personal helicopter embellished with gold "T"'s, and now sitting in this palatial penthouse, it began to sink in how some very fortunate people enjoyed a level of wealth and power far beyond my imagination.

Mike Tyson reached over and shook my hand. "You did it, right?

I nodded sheepishly, and he grinned widely in response. He ended his telephone call, snapped his fingers, and a tall black man, the butler, appeared from nowhere.

"Rudy's gonna drive my shit. Make sure you take care of him."

I got up, expecting to follow the butler, but my new boss motioned for me to remain seated.

"Relax, enjoy yourself. It's going to be fun for you. We need a limo. We've gotta buy some limos. I fired all my drivers. I had them all over the place. They're all fired. You're my driver now. You're gonna be in full control and in charge of all my cars. You're gonna travel with me wherever I go."

He told Caesar that Ouie had to move out and go to a hotel. Instead, I would take over his bedroom. He also instructed Caesar to show me around town and buy me all the clothes I needed for the next two weeks.

"You won't have to go back to the City."

Ouie was one of Tyson's closest childhood friends from Brownsville. Ouie told me later that I must be pretty important for him to get kicked out of that bedroom.

Before Caesar and I made it to the door, Tyson called out. "And Caesar, take Rudy down to the garage later. I don't even know what I got. Everybody's been playing around with my shit. Go downstairs and straighten my shit out. Make it pretty."

In the elevator descending to the lobby, Caesar said: "Listen, Rudy, everything is a mess. But don't worry about it right now. Let's get you some clothes first."

We went to the garage to get Caesar's jeep, and I asked him which of the large array of luxury cars belonged to my new boss.

Caesar chuckled. "They all belong to MT."

I couldn't believe it. I expected that Tyson owned two or three cars besides the grey fourteen-pack Mercedes limo. Caesar pointed out twenty expensive vehicles, all dirty, some with flat tires, others with body damage. I told Caesar that I wanted to go right away to an auto supply store and buy shampoo, wax, and detailing items. He reminded me that Tyson wanted me to get some clothes and become familiar with Atlantic City before anything else. I protested loudly, and Caesar finally gave in.

We returned thirty minutes later, and I took off my shirt and got to work washing, waxing, and cleaning Tyson's automobile collection. I also organized everything I found inside, including dozens of audio and video cassettes. Six hours later Mike Tyson came looking for me. He was dressed in his favorite white sweat shorts. I heard him yelling my name as he entered the garage with Caesar.

"Rudy, what are you doing?"

"I'm getting it all together, sir."

"Forget about it. Don't do that shit all at once. Come on and hang out with us."

"No, I want to finish this first."

Tyson turned to Caesar. "You see, first day on the job, and he's taking care of everything."

I worked until around 2 a.m. because I wanted my new boss to see all of his vehicles clean and sparkling by the morning. Finally, I made it to the bedroom and was ready to conk out. Within the past twelve hours I had quit my job at UPS, flown in Donald Trump's private helicopter to Atlantic City, been hired formally by Mike Tyson to be his driver wherever he went, and cleaned and waxed his entire inventory of luxury automobiles. Caesar heard me next door and came in.

"You better get some rest, Rudy," he said. "MT gets up at five to go running. You've gotta follow us in case we need the car."

***

At 5 a.m. sharp Caesar woke me up and told me to hurry. Tyson was already in his sweats anxious to hit the street. Caesar told me to grab the keys to one of the cars and meet them in front of the building. I threw on some clothes and jumped in the express elevator. The black Jaguar looked pretty inviting so I fired it up and sped up the ramp to street level. Tyson already was half-way down the street with Caesar not far behind.

The sun hadn't yet risen before Tyson finished five miles at a brisk pace. When we returned to the penthouse, Chef Early was cooking away in the kitchen. He was a tall, white-haired, very distinguished-looking black man in his sixties whose specialty was making soul food. Chef Early had cooked for many celebrities, including Michael Jackson and Whitney Houston. For breakfast he typically served up eggs along with low-fat turkey sausages and assorted fruits and juices. Tyson would have a big breakfast including, without fail, a bowl of his favorite cereal, Cap'n Crunch, then go back to sleep until 11 a.m. In the late afternoon he would hit the gym and do his boxing workout. In the evening, he would spend some time on the treadmill, Stair-Master, Gravitron, or stationary bike. This was the daily regimen that Mike Tyson followed and enjoyed and which, by the time I started working for him, had made him the heavyweight champion of the world.

Caesar told me I was dismissed until MT woke up. I went down to the garage, applied Armor All to the vinyl and leather surfaces in each of the cars, and made a list of broken items I had discovered the night before. I realized Tyson was standing behind me, shaking his head in disbelief because his entire automobile collection was clean and shiny for the first time since he could remember. I showed him all of his compact discs, audio and video cassettes, and even packs of chewing gum, had been organized and placed in one bag so that he could take all of his stuff with him regardless which car he was using.

"I can't believe this." He slapped me on the back so hard he almost knocked me to the ground. "You know how to drive a stick?"

Tyson told me to pull out the red Lamborghini Countach. When I started it up, it sounded like a small jet.

"We're gonna go to the City for the afternoon."

I attempted to let the clutch out slowly, but I hadn't anticipated the massive power of this vehicle's twelve cylinders and five-hundred horses. The Countach sprang forward uncontrollably and, when I slammed on the brakes, it died. I apologized to my boss, but Tyson just laughed, assuring me that I'd get the hang of it. As we exited the garage, several people saw us and shouted "Mike, Mike!" I grabbed the Jersey Turnpike and headed for New York City. Tyson insisted we drive at 90 miles-per-hour all the way, and we never got stopped. One of Tyson's great loves was traveling on the road at high speeds. We were in midtown Manhattan in little over an hour.

On Madison Avenue Tyson visited several stores while I remained outside. After that we headed for his old neighborhood. As we cruised slowly through the streets of the Brownsville section of Brooklyn, people screamed out his name. Tyson told me to stop from time to time so he could get out and visit with old friends on the stoops of housing projects and at a park. I noticed that many times Mike Tyson handed out cash. After five hours in the City, he told me he was tired. He was in training for the Pinklon Thomas fight scheduled for May 30, 1987 at the Las Vegas Hilton. Soon we were roaring down the Jersey Turnpike on our way back to Atlantic City and Tyson's penthouse at the Ocean Club.

Mike Tyson's life was healthy and organized during those first few months I was with him in Atlantic City. Kevin Rooney, his main trainer for a number of years, was a strict disciplinarian who made sure his fighter was in bed by a certain hour and followed a carefully-planned diet. When Tyson had an 11 p.m. curfew, Rooney would be at our door at 11:15 p.m. to check for compliance. If I didn't get my boss home on time, I would get yelled at. When Rooney suspected that Tyson was sneaking snacks at night, we came home one evening to find a chain and lock around the refrigerator and a note taped to it: "Sorry, Mike, not until 8 a.m." Sometimes Rooney would leave his fighter a pitcher of ice water and an apple or a pear with a note: "Love, Kevin."

Even though his role was full-time "enforcer," it was clear that Kevin Rooney genuinely cared about Mike Tyson. After training sessions, Rooney would have long talks with him, and he would swing by with movies and popcorn if he detected Tyson was feeling down or bored. Rooney tried to be like a brother to him. If we let Rooney down, we felt bad because he was such a good man. He instilled a sense of "team playing" for all who worked with him. And the team was playing for the single goal of making Michael Gerard Tyson the undisputed heavyweight champion of the world.

As time passed I learned that there was a very real tradition behind the fight jacket Mike Tyson left for me at

Trump Air the day I quit my job at UPS. Kevin Rooney represented that tradition which began in 1979. That was the year Cus D'Amato rescued twelve-year-old Tyson from the Tryon School for Boys, an infamous juvenile reformatory in Johnstown, New York. Kevin Rooney was one of the last individuals who was able to carry on that tradition before things started going very badly for Mike Tyson.

I never had the opportunity to meet Cus D'Amato because he died from pneumonia on November 4, 1985, one year before I met Mike Tyson. But Kevin Rooney and two other trainers, Steve Lott and Matt Baranski, often recalled how Cus would have handled a particular training technique or other issue troubling them. It wasn't long before I felt like I personally had known this boxing legend.

There is little doubt that the character "Mickey" in the *Rocky* movies was based in part on Cus D'Amato's life. D'Amato fell in love with boxing as a child and made it his life-long career. In the thirties, he was a boxing coach in the army. He lived for more than three decades at his Gramercy Gym, located on Manhattan's Lower East Side, while Camille Ewald, his Ukranian-born companion for nearly fifty years, maintained a home in upstate New York. The Gramercy Gym produced champions Rocky Graziano, Floyd Patterson, and Jose Torres, the last two trained by Cus D'Amato.

D'Amato suffered from several medical conditions. For one thing, he was color-blind. When he was twelve, he got into a street fight and injured his right eye from which he never would see clearly again. By early middle-age, D'Amato practically had lost the senses of smell and taste. But he had an extremely strong will and was a workaholic, an unrelenting drill sergeant who pushed his boxing students toward perfection. It was from Cus D'Amato that Tyson got into the habit of 5 a.m. five-mile jogs, afternoon training sessions, and evening workouts on the machines. D'Amato also was fearless, standing up at great personal risk to mobsters Frankie Carbo and Blinky Palermo who had attempted to wedge themselves into the world of professional boxing. That was why Cus D'Amato had developed the irritating habit of constantly looking over his shoulder in restaurants and other public places.

After years of living at the Gramercy Gym, Cus D'Amato finally made the move to upstate New York to live full-time with Camille Ewald. They had purchased an old house with three storeys and seven bedrooms next to the Hudson River in the sleepy town of Catskill. It wasn't long before they began taking in troubled kids to fill that big house, especially those in whom Cus D'Amato saw a potential professional fighter. Two miles away, above the police station on Main Street, D'Amato set up the only gym in the area to teach kids the sport of boxing.

Fate would have it that in 1978 the State of New York decided to transfer unrepentant, habitual-offender Michael Gerard Tyson out of New York City's Spofford Juvenile Detention Center to the Tryon School, a much-harsher reformatory in Johnstown. Despite the severe discipline imposed on the young inmates there, Tyson continued to act out of control. Then one day he noticed a poster of a boxer on the wall of the gym and realized the school's athletic coach, Bobby Stewart, was that fighter. After Tyson proved to Stewart that he really had changed his ways, the former professional welterweight agreed to give him some lessons.

It didn't take long for Bobby Stewart to conclude his

young student was somebody with extraordinary raw talent and physical ability. He decided to introduce young Tyson to Cus D'Amato who lived in nearby Catskill. A short time later he was negotiating with the Department of Corrections to get Tyson released to his custody. In 1979, Tyson went to live at The White House where other kids had been taken in by Cus and Camille. From that point on, D'Amato began training Tyson to be a professional boxer. In 1984, Tyson was a National Golden Gloves winner and soon would become the youngest heavyweight champion of the world. When I met Tyson, he already was unbeaten in twenty-eight bouts, twenty-six of them by knockouts.

Mike Tyson didn't have any relationship with his natural father, Jimmy Kirkpatrick. Cus D'Amato filled that role when he brought Tyson into his home. After Tyson's mother, Lorna, died of cancer, D'Amato formally adopted him. Camille Ewald told the story that one afternoon Mike Tyson brought home a friend and introduced her as his mother. The kid looked at Tyson, then at her, then back at him, shaking his head and walking away totally confused. Tyson also had several "brothers" while he was at The White House, Jay Bright, Tom Patti, and others for whom Cus and Camille had opened their doors. There is a home video of them sitting around the dining table, and you can see in Mike Tyson's expression how happy he was to be a part of this multi-racial family.

Cus D'Amato believed the real power of the fighter was in his mind more than in his fists. That's why he spent so much time speaking with the youngster who came to live with him in 1979. D'Amato needed to find out what was going on inside that very disturbed head, praying that he could redirect all the negative energy to the sport of boxing, and in the process save this kid from a life of crime and premature death. His talks with Mike Tyson, as well as with others whom he guided over the years, included his admonition that too much money and women-chasing were evils which destroyed the strength and purity of the professional athlete.

Cus D'Amato was convinced from the first day that Bobby Stewart brought young Tyson to him that he had a future heavyweight champion on his hands. And so, from the very beginning, he carefully surrounded Mike Tyson with those who shared D'Amato's values and beliefs, and who had Tyson's welfare, both personal and professional, as their number one concern. This was the tradition Cus put into motion in 1979, a tradition embodied in the fight jacket Mike Tyson left for me at Trump Air when I was headed to Atlantic City to start working full-time for him. It wasn't about the money. At the beginning very few conversations involved that subject. We were a family. Sadly, this tradition was to come to a close within a couple of years. During my first year with him, Mike Tyson seemed to take his fabulous earnings in stride. He very much enjoyed returning to his old Brownsville neighborhood, sitting on tenement stoops or in the park and joking with old friends.

"Treat people right, Rudy," my boss told me. "Don't let this shit get to you." Tyson was referring to his money, luxury cars, and other material possessions.

Mike Tyson was very concerned about the living conditions of black people in this country, especially the children, and wanted to do something about it.

"What is important is caring about people. Even if I

got a billion dollars, I'm still gonna be known as little Mike."
It was his way of saying he would never grow larger than life.

If Mike Tyson saw people on the street who looked
desperate, he would tell me to stop, bolt out of the limo and
hand them some cash. He never carried anything less than
$100 bills. I saw him hand out $100 bills to hundreds of
kids. We would get the cash at Bill Cayton's office after
signing receipts to keep track of the outflow. I would use
paperclips to divide the bills into $1,000 packs so my boss
would know how much dough he had with him.

On the average Mike Tyson would carry around
$25,000 in cash in case he wanted to stop and buy something.
He was an impulse shopper. One summer day in 1987, we
were on Atlantic Avenue in Brooklyn, and we passed by A.J.
Lester's. He told me to stop the limo, and he went inside the
store where he bought ten-dozen pairs of sneakers of all
sizes. We loaded up the limo and drove around Brownsville,
handing them out to needy kids on the street. Tyson liked to
play with these poor kids and, during that first summer, I
recall we had a lot of spontaneous touch-football games.

This is when Mike Tyson seemed happiest during the
years I worked for him. He wanted to make people feel that
he was just a normal guy from his neighborhood who had
never forgotten his people. It didn't bother MT back then
that the media might not appreciate the fact he wasn't doing
a whole lot of glamorous things.

One day approximately eight months after I started
working full-time for him, Mike Tyson turned to me.

"Hey, man, have I ever paid you?"

Although all my basic needs, food, clothing, shelter,
and transportation had been taken care of so far, I never had

received a paycheck.

"No, sir, we never discussed this. I don't know if I'm getting paid."

Mike Tyson looked at me in amazement. This was further proof to him I wasn't after his money. After that day, I was placed on the payroll at $300 a week. My first check included payment for all the time I had been working for him since May of 1987.

Some of the original members of Team Tyson were still in place when I started working full-time for MT. The trainers were Kevin Rooney, Matt Baranski, and Steve Lott, and Jim Jacobs and Bill Cayton were Tyson's co-managers. They had developed a game plan for Mike Tyson which propelled him from an amateur to a world champion in less than two years, making him a very rich man by age twenty. Jacobs was a long-time friend of D'Amato and former champion handball player. Jacobs was a collector and, among other things, he had acquired the world's largest collection of fight films. Tyson spent hundreds of hours in his attic room at The White House studying those films. When D'Amato died at the end of 1985, Jacobs became the man in whom Mike Tyson placed his greatest trust until Jacobs himself died in the spring of 1988.

As Cus D'Amato's health rapidly deteriorated in the mid-eighties, he used to say the only reason he had to keep on living was to see the day when his "son" would become heavyweight champion of the world. D'Amato passed away before that day came, but he had been able to see Tyson win eleven professional fights, all of them by knockouts. The aging, legendary trainer, who transformed Mike Tyson into the unbeatable heavyweight fighting machine that he became, never took credit for his success.

"I just discover and uncover," Cus D'Amato used to say about his fighters. "They do all the rest."

On May 30, 1987, Mike Tyson was scheduled to fight Pinklon Thomas at the Las Vegas Hilton. The match would be Tyson's defense of both the WBC and WBA heavyweight titles. Because there was still a lot to do to put the inventory of cars back in mint condition, MT decided to leave me in Atlantic City. In the sixth round of the fight, Tyson knocked out Thomas and was back at the Ocean Club the next day.

Things were quiet for awhile because the next fight was scheduled for August 1, also at the Las Vegas Hilton, against Tony Tucker, the IBF heavyweight champion. Kevin Rooney kept MT on a very tight leash during those two months, calling reveille each day at 5 a.m for him to suit up for his morning run. In the afternoons, Rooney and the other trainers would get him on the light and heavy bags and then watch him spar with other boxers.

Tyson's training sessions included Cus D'Amato's specialized techniques. One in particular was designed to develop Tyson's trademark rapid-fire bobbing and weaving. Because he was shorter than many heavyweights, Cus knew that Tyson would have to be able to "hide out" for awhile, bobbing and weaving from side to side, until he could get in close enough and use uppercut or roundhouse punches with devastating effect. Kevin Rooney would tie a gold ball to a long string, then suspend it from the ceiling. Setting it in motion like a pendulum, MT would have to move quickly from side to side and up and down to avoid getting bopped on the head. Rooney would pick up the speed and send it in different directions, and Tyson would dip, bob, and weave faster and faster. Training methods, like this one, seemed to give Mike Tyson an edge over his opponents.

The Ocean Club had an exercise room with treadmills, stationary bikes, StairMasters, and a Gravitron. Rooney would swing by and make sure MT faithfully was performing his evening workout. Obesity ran in Tyson's family which caused everybody to be concerned, including my boss, about unchecked weight gain. Rodney, Tyson's older brother, weighed 280 pounds by age eleven. Denise, his sister, died from an obesity-related heart attack in her mid-twenties. Rooney and the other trainers meticulously calculated the proper daily caloric intake for their charge and worked closely with the cook to develop low-fat meals. Chef Early whipped up a lot of innovative turkey dishes. I noticed MT's pained expression whenever he watched fast-food commercials displaying ribs, cheeseburgers, and fried chicken. But as long as Mike Tyson could have his "CK," Cap'n Crunch, every morning, life was bearable. He ate that cereal dry, and it made his stomach feel very full.

As his full-time chauffeur, I was with Tyson 24/7. One day Kevin Rooney pulled me aside and instructed me to report back to him if my boss wanted to do something which would violate his strict training program. Back then Tyson usually was happy just relaxing after each of his three daily workouts listening to music or watching videos. MT had all of Billie Holiday's recordings and an extensive rap music collection. Tyson's videos consisted mainly of martial arts movies, like *Fists of Fury*, and cartoon characters "Tom and Jerry" and "The Roadrunner."

From time to time co-managers Bill Cayton and Jim Jacobs would meet with Tyson and describe his financial situation and the steps they had taken to protect his wealth. If they needed him to pay a bill, they would explain in detail the reason for the expenditure. Cayton and Jacobs also made me aware that no craziness was allowed in the Tyson camp. All members of the Team were working toward the same goal, to ensure that Mike Tyson's career kept moving ahead on a safe and profitable course.

When I wasn't driving him around, I spent a lot of time taking care of Tyson's cars, making sure everything was in order. He appeared very pleased with what was happening with his automobile collection. Because I was in charge now, Tyson told everybody who wanted to use one of the vehicles that they would have to speak with me. I would tell whoever wanted to take one of them out for a drive that there was something wrong with it. This way very few cars left the garage unless either me or MT was driving it. This system greatly relieved Tyson who hated saying "no" to friends and family, but for me it was easy.

Two months later, Tyson returned to the Las Vegas Hilton where he won a twelve-round unanimous decision against Tony Tucker. This victory added the IBF title to his WBC and WBA titles. Mike Tyson now was the proud owner of the heavyweight belts from all three recognized boxing associations.

Although he seemed to appreciate my hard work, professionalism, and courtesy, there were times that Mike Tyson yelled at me while we lived in Atlantic City. For one thing, my boss didn't like repeating instructions. However, by that point in my life, I had met enough rich people to realize they didn't have a lot of patience for anything. I also knew that most of the rich occasionally yelled at their help.

It was part of a power display they believed necessary to prevent people from taking advantage of them.

Mike Tyson had been treating me fairly and kindly on a daily basis long enough for me to know that he truly appreciated me being part of the Team. Once in awhile, when things really got to him, I would see MT down in the garage conducting an inspection of his "fleet." He was looking for dirt or other potential problems with his cars, but he never found any. Sometimes Tyson would storm away, mumbling, "Man, I can't ever get anything on you."

Kevin Rooney always reminded me about one of Cus D'Amato's sayings: "Don't do what the champion wants you to do, just do what's right for the champion." During the more than five years I worked for him, Mike Tyson fired me twice for refusing to obey his instructions. I had refused because what he had asked me to do was against his best interests. Each time Tyson hired me back right away. By putting his welfare above all else, my boss realized that I had become a loyal member of the Team Tyson Tradition, the tradition represented by The Jacket bearing my name.

"Gotta Have It Givens"

"Gotta-Have-It-Givens"

As time marched on "Iron Mike" Tyson continued to earn increasingly fabulous sums of money. This caused a significant rise in the anxiety level of co-managers Jim Jacobs and Bill Cayton. While Mike Tyson was in training, the strict D'Amato-Rooney regimen kept him on the straight and narrow. In 1985, between March 6 and December 27, Tyson had fifteen heavyweight bouts. Between January 11 and November 22, 1986, he had thirteen fights. The result was that, in fewer than two years, Mike Tyson had severely depleted the stable of heavyweight boxers. Consequently, in 1987 he only had four fights, picking up the WBA and IBF heavyweight titles that year.

Jacobs and Cayton understood the more free time Mike Tyson had on his hands the more likely he was to get into trouble. He had become rich and famous, his face recognized in every corner of the globe. This caused his co-managers to become very concerned about the "groupie syndrome." They were afraid Tyson wouldn't be able to handle all the new-found attention and affection. They made it clear to me and Caesar that part of our job was to protect Mike Tyson from the multitudes of crazy women and gold diggers who would derail his boxing career.

Jacobs and Cayton instructed us to stay nearby at all times even while Tyson was having sex. They explained the truth, unfortunately, was whatever a judge or jury *believed*, not what really had happened. To protect Mike Tyson from false accusations and frivolous lawsuits, he needed somebody to be with him at all times to observe what really was going on. The presence of another person also sent a message to Tyson's companions: don't invent stories because we're here too, just outside the door, even looking in on you from time to time. I gave deposition testimony on several occasions about what I personally had seen going on between my boss and a groupie sex partner. After my depositions were taken, the accusers did not pursue their cases. Tyson didn't need a full-time bodyguard to protect him as much as he needed a round-the-clock witness.

Tyson told me that, when he was a youngster, the girls were scared of him. While growing up in Brownsville, he never had a girlfriend. Now that he had a lot of money, it wasn't just his co-managers who believed women would be trying to take advantage of him. But even though he said "all women were alike," Mike Tyson still was looking for a girl who really wanted him and not his money.

When I joined Team Tyson in May of 1987, MT mainly was seeing three women, Naomi Campbell, Suzette Charles, and Robin Givens. Campbell was one of the world's top models who lived in a luxurious Manhattan penthouse. Charles was a former Miss America who lived in Cherry Hill, New Jersey. Robin Givens was a television actress starring in the ABC sitcom *Head of the Class*.

"Don't let the girls cross paths," Bill Cayton warned me. He believed that a tug-of-war was underway among these three ladies, the prize, exclusive possession of Mike Tyson. Jacobs and Cayton were afraid an ugly cat fight might break out if these three women got too close to each other at one of the boxing matches so I had to make sure each was seated far enough away from the others.

I drove Mike Tyson and Naomi Campbell around dozens of times during 1987. They were a strange mix. She was very polished, having been raised and educated in Italy and England. In her crisp British accent, Campbell talked down to Tyson all the time, attempting to "educate" him, correcting his grammar and teaching him manners. She also got him into a designer-clothes mentality by taking him on costly shopping trips to expensive boutiques on Madison and Fifth Avenues. Until then Tyson had been wearing clothes mostly from A. J. Lester's, a Brooklyn sporting-goods store. Naomi Campbell got MT interested in clothing from Gianni Versace, the designer for whom she did most of her modeling work. Tyson's wardrobe eventually became almost exclusively Versace, including $2,500 sport shirts and $5,000 leather pants.

Tyson would shower Naomi Campbell with very expensive gold and diamond jewelry. There were a number of times I picked her up from Philadelphia International, the closest major airport to Atlantic City. Campbell usually was on a tight schedule so, instead of having time for a real date, many times I would just drive MT and her to Manhattan. This gave them several hours to have sex in the limousine. The movement those two generated back there was incredible. Sometimes I thought the car, rocking and rolling, was going to tip over. When we arrived at Naomi Campbell's building, they would say their goodbyes.

"You know, Mike, if it wasn't for the sex, I wouldn't even talk to you," she seemed to enjoy telling him. "You don't offer me anything else."

My boss would just laugh. Exhausted frm the non-stop sexual encounter, he would sleep all the way back to the Ocean Club in Atlantic City.

Naomi Campbell thoroughly enjoyed Mike Tyson's sexual abilities during those rides in the back of the limousine. I had heard enough hours of her screams and shrieks of ecstacy to be certain of that. As I drove them from Atlantic City to Manhattan, MT transported her to a different planet. It was a place far away from that to which she had become accustomed in her profession where there were a lot of polite, refined people not known for their sexual prowess. Eventually, Naomi Campbell got bored with Tyson and, at that point, he began focusing more of his attention on the two remaining women in his life.

Suzette Charles was a stark contrast to the tall, black super-model from England. Charles was more caring and understanding when she was with Tyson. Although a very nice "apple-pie" type, she also seemed to enjoy the "bad-boy" image of her tough, ghetto-bred boyfriend. It was as if Mike Tyson stirred in her feelings she had suppressed in her very prim and proper middle-American existence. In the back of the limousine, there were a lot of chicken-in-the-bucket dinners followed by wild sex.

Tyson and Charles had a nice relationship which lasted all the way to the Desiree Washington incident a few years later. Don King, the infamous boxing promoter with the electrified hair, had been circling Mike Tyson like a buzzard since 1987. King realized back then that the only real heavyweight meal ticket in town had MT's name written all over it. Tyson had been knocking out each and every one of King's fighters. As part of his master plan to win Tyson's affection and unquestioned loyalty, Don King hired Suzette Charles as a spokesperson for some of the fights he was promoting. Tyson heard a rumor that King had been sleeping with Charles. He felt betrayed, but like he would be able to do so many times in the coming years, Don King convinced Tyson the rumor was false.

Mike Tyson loved to give expensive presents to his girlfriends, jewelry, designer clothes and, sometimes, even automobiles. But no matter how sincere they appeared to act toward him, deep down Tyson still believed that all women really were after his money instead of him. The more beautiful the women were, the more insecurity they generated for him, including the thought they might be having sex with other men while he was spending great sums of money on them. MT worried a lot about what his pretty women were doing when they weren't around him.

Although he dated glamorous ladies who were in the news, MT never stopped being with ordinary girls from his old neighborhood and others wherever he met them. He seemed more at ease with them than with celebrities. Tyson was very self-conscious about his lack of formal education and high-pitched, lisping voice. In almost every city we visited, we would pass through the red-light district, but only to watch the spectacle, never to reach out and touch someone. Occasionally, Tyson would have some fun with the hookers, rolling down the window so they would be able to catch a glimpse of him. Once they recognized him, these women would scream and run after us as we pulled away. One night we caused a small riot on 42nd Street in New York City. As his window descended, Tyson called out to a group of ladies of the night.

"Hey, how can a brother get some ass around here?" MT shouted out.

When they saw who the potential client was, a huge army of pimps and hookers emerged from nowhere, the girls flashing body parts and chasing us for the better part of two blocks. Tyson got a big laugh out of that spectacle.

I had seen my boss with some very beautiful white women, like Las Vegas showgirls, but they never triggered jealousy in him. That feeling only applied to black women. This was demonstrated to me clearly as the result of an incident in the spring of 1991. MT had a girlfriend from Los Angeles named Hope. She was very beautiful with very big tits and a tremendous sexual appetite. The three things that Hope said most often were "yes," "yes," and "oh, yes!" She wanted to do the wild thing with me, but if I had accepted that offer, it would have marked the end of my career working for Tyson. If MT suspected somebody was getting it on with one of his girls, they were out of his life for good. Tyson gave you just enough rope to hang yourself, and I wasn't about to mess things up. I could tell that MT was still puzzled after all this time by not being able "to get anything" on me. When he sent me to get gas or run an errand, I returned right away. He would tell me to take some time off, but then I wouldn't go anywhere.

"You're always around, Rudy," he would say and then shake his head.

Mike Tyson wasn't used to this type of loyalty. Too many people already had taken advantage of him during his rapid rise to fame and fortune. He would demonstrate his gratitude for my respect and loyalty by always giving me the customary hug. Sometimes that hug turned into a half-nelson, dragging me along for awhile as he kept on walking. Mike Tyson knew that he could count on me to be there for him at all times.

One night after Hope had visited Tyson in his Los Angeles apartment, my boss told me to follow her. She left earlier than usual, telling him she had to visit a friend. MT wanted me to find out where Hope went, if she made any calls or met up with anybody, basically everything she did after leaving the apartment. I took the black Lamborghini Diablo and began following her at a discreet distance. She stopped at Roscoe's House of Chicken and Waffles, a soul-food restaurant, got out of her car, and walked over to a black Lexus. She spoke for a few moments with the male driver, and then they went inside the restaurant. The other person was actor Wesley Snipes.

Mike Tyson was paging me. I called him back and let him know the situation. He told me to go inside and see what was happening. Hope was sitting on Snipes' lap. Once my boss learned that Hope was "involved" with another guy, I suspected things were going to happen very quickly. Less than ten minutes later Mike Tyson pulled up in the yellow Ferrari Testarossa. My boss was with our new bodyguard, Anthony Pitts, a former professional football player who stood six-seven and weighed two-fifty. Tyson jumped out of the Ferrari.

Anthony Pitts looked over at me and said: "There's gonna be trouble."

We followed quickly behind our boss. When they caught sight of Mike Tyson, the famous actor froze, Hope falling out his lap onto the floor.

"Now, Mike, Mike, we can do this together. I don't

want no problems," Snipes said, waving his hand.

"Let's go in the bathroom!" Tyson snapped. "Rudy, put Hope in the car."

When I returned from the parking lot, I noticed Anthony Pitts was blocking the bathroom door. A couple of minutes later we heard a loud noise inside, and then Tyson emerged alone.

"Gimme' the keys to the Diablo," he mumbled.

After Mike Tyson was gone, I slowly cracked open the bathroom door. Wesley Snipes was sitting on the floor against the far wall, head tilted to one side, unconscious.

***

In 1986 Mike Tyson met Robin Givens, a television actress two years his senior. Givens continued to show her interest in the champ by attending his May 30, 1987 Pinklon Thomas fight in Las Vegas. After that fight, MT had two months before he would meet his next opponent, Tony Tucker, for the IBF title. My boss spent a lot of time with Givens during that period of time. As the year progressed, it was clear that Mike Tyson was more interested in Robin Givens than anyone else.

There was no future for Tyson with super-model Naomi Campbell who represented one extreme. She was completely independent, very wealthy, and a big celebrity in her own right. Suzette Charles was gorgeous, polite, and caring, but her fifteen minutes of fame as a former Miss America was over. At that point in time Robin Givens presented herself to Tyson as the perfect compromise. She was well-known but not a megastar. She was nice but had a feisty personality which made MT identify more easily with her than Suzette. And Tyson saw Givens as one of the most beautiful black women he had ever set eyes on. After he had been with her a few months, it was obvious that my boss had fallen for Robin Givens in a big way. MT couldn't believe that somebody so beautiful wanted to be with him.

I met Robin Givens for the first time when MT sent me to pick her up at Philadelphia International and take her to the Ocean Club. It was clear from the beginning she wasn't thrilled that MT's full-time chauffeur was a Puerto Rican. Givens told me that she didn't like Spanish people, claiming her father was Hispanic and had abandoned the family when she was little. There were to be no courtesies or "thanks" coming in my direction from Robin Givens. Instead, I was just someone who opened doors for her. It looked like she was going to be a witch from the start.

Before she married Tyson, Robin Givens showed herself to be a very skilled tease. MT was fascinated with her virgin-like innocence. Givens put on a great "shy girl" act which made Tyson feel in control unlike when he was in the presence of the very self-confident Naomi Campbell.

"Did I kiss good, Mike?" Givens would ask him innocently. It was easy to see this was all part of a grand production. However, it wasn't my place to interfere with my boss's personal life. I had heard that Givens had been hanging out with Eddie Murphy, certainly no saint, and that she had developed a reputation as somewhat of a groupie back in LA where she filmed *Head of the Class*.

There came a time when Robin Givens believed she finally had conquered the undefeated heavyweight champ. It was then that she let her guard down, revealing some of her true stripes. When that happened, even though he continued to act like a fool in love when he was around her, Mike

Tyson resisted the idea of tying the knot.

"She has wanted me to marry her for a long time," he said, "but I ain't gonna do it. Hey, I'm only twenty-one, and I want to play the field for awhile. Besides, we fight all the time. She thinks she is so much better than me just because she's had an education. It may be true, but I hate the way she goes about telling me. I retaliate by telling her I am the heavyweight champion, and she should know her place. Man, she really gets into a temper at that and comes at me. She knows she can't hurt me if she kicks me in the head so she tries to kick me in the groin."

Robin Givens knew that she had to pull out all the stops to be able to land Mike Tyson for herself. She had become well-aware of Camille Ewald's powerful influence over her son. One day she reached out to Camille at The White House, her goal to get Tyson's elderly surrogate mother signed up with the Robin Givens program.

"She was upset about Mike and other girls," Camille related later. "I told her, Mike is young. He's a champion. He doesn't know how to say 'no.' He may see other girls, and he may let them kiss him, but that doesn't mean he goes to bed with them."

Robin Givens responded to Camille's explanation by stating that she was "not one of his bimbos."

***

On January 22, 1988, Mike Tyson was scheduled to defend his three heavyweight titles against the challenger, Larry Holmes, a former heavyweight champ, at the Atlantic City Convention Center. Tyson was looking for his thirty-third straight victory. In the fourth round, Tyson knocked Holmes to the canvas three times before the referee intervened and stopped the fight. With yet another Tyson knockout victory, there was great celebration in the elegant ballroom of the Trump Plaza.

However, something very big had been brewing for a few weeks prior to the fight which radically would change Mike Tyson's life forever. I didn't know it at the time, but it was to be the beginning of the end. The whole process would take nearly four years to play out, but the wheels already had been set in motion. Self-styled businesswoman Ruth Roper, Robin Givens' mother, informed Tyson's co-managers their fighter had gotten her daughter pregnant.

During the night of February 7, 1988, I took Mike Tyson and Robin Givens to the home of a Catholic priest, Father George Clements, who performed their marriage ceremony. They had met the priest earlier that evening while attending the NBA All-Star Game at Chicago Stadium. I was driving the Mercedes 500SEL limousine with 18K gold rims. All of its knobs and buttons and the exterior emblems of the vehicle were studded with diamonds. Two days later Ruth Roper called Mike Tyson's co-managers and warned them that, if they didn't take steps right away to make the "religious ceremony" a legal marriage, then she would get the couple formally hitched in Nevada. The next day Tyson and Givens arrived at Manhattan's Municipal Building for a civil proceeding to legalize their union. On St. Valentine's Day, Tyson's new mother-in-law threw a ritzy party for a small group at the Helmsley Palace Hotel on Madison Avenue.

Tyson assigned Caesar and James Anderson to protect Robin Givens. He dispatched me to Atlantic City to clean and organize the Ocean Club penthouse. After that I was instructed to go to Catskill, pick up the training team, and check on Camille who had undergone hip surgery. As soon as I arrived there, Kevin Rooney and I discussed our boss getting married to Givens. The morning after the religious ceremony at Father Clements' house, MT called Camille to inform her about her new daughter-in-law. By that time I had seen too many fights between the couple. I also was aware that Tyson resented Givens' growing bossiness so I was disappointed that he had chosen her to be his first wife. Camille announced the wedding celebration would continue at The White House.

When I next saw my boss, he gave me the customary hug and asked how his mother was doing. He also wanted to know about his pigeons. Ever since he was a child, like many ghetto kids, Tyson loved these birds. He kept more than two-hundred pigeons at The White House, including some very rare ones. I noticed the huge wedding ring on Givens' finger. It was the size of a golf ball. Tyson was wearing a simple wedding band. I drove the newlyweds, Cayton, Rooney, Lott, and Rory Holloway back to the Catskills for the continuation of the wedding festivities. Cayton had bad chemistry with Holloway, one of Tyson's closest friends. Holloway had started hanging around all the time. For some reason Bill Cayton had a gut feeling that Holloway was going to be a bad influence on his fighter.

Mike Tyson sat in the front with me all the way to The White House listening to rap music. He appeared to be genuinely happy to be married. There was no doubt that he was very much in love with Robin Givens even though their relationship over the past few months had turned from mostly tranquil to frequently argumentative. MT had found the missing link in his life. He had amassed great fame and fortune so far in his professional boxing career. Now he was adding to it a permanent relationship with the girl of his dreams. Tyson also was very excited about two properties Givens had told him they should be considering to purchase as their main residence, one of which was the Vanderbilt Mansion in Bernardsville, New Jersey. He also mentioned that he wanted to buy a Rolls Royce limousine, an idea his new wife enthusiastically embraced.

During the ride up to the Catskills, MT patted me on the back. "You're doing a good job, Rudy."

I never tried to be Mike Tyson's friend or get involved in his private life. The idea that I should "know my place" did not offend me. I was just very grateful for the opportunity to work for this champion, especially the more I learned about the Tyson Tradition and the more people I met along the way who were part of it. Despite what I had seen and heard, I was determined to keep to myself the bad feelings I had been developing about Robin Givens. If this marriage was going to survive, Tyson and Givens were going to need all the support they could get. At all times I respected their privacy, hiding out in my room whenever they didn't need me to chauffeur them around, run errands, or provide security.

***

Events had moved too swiftly for co-managers Jim Jacobs and Bill Cayton, the people who carefully and fairly had managed Mike Tyson's business affairs after he turned pro in 1985. However, there had not been sufficient time to discuss with their fighter the very important matter of a prenuptial agreement. MT might have raced to the altar as a result of being tricked. Maybe Robin Givens really wasn't pregnant. There were too many questions which remained unanswered at the worst possible time for the co-managers: both were dealing with severe health problems. Jim Jacobs recently had undergone intestinal surgery. Bill Cayton was in the hospital for inflammation of the heart membranes. Within days after the marriage between Mike Tyson and Robin Givens, their worst fears began to materialize. Through her attorney, Givens' mother demanded the co-managers immediately turn over documents relating to their handling of Mike Tyson.

Mike Tyson didn't know much, or even care, about this struggle for control over his financial affairs. We were in Japan preparing for the Tony Tubbs fight scheduled for March 21 at the Tokyo Dome. The newlyweds used part of this time to have the honeymoon they hadn't taken so far. They were able to do a lot of sightseeing in limousines provided by companies promoting the match, and those companies also provided the couple security personnel. Yet, it was during this trip to Japan that my boss decided to assign me duties beyond being his full-time chauffeur. He made me his personal assistant, knowing from my prior service that I would get results quickly and professionally. MT also wanted me to serve as an additional bodyguard.

After awhile, the new Mrs. Tyson headed back to the States to immerse herself in finalizing the deal to purchase the Vanderbilt Mansion in Bernardsville, New Jersey. We later learned there had been a big ruckus at Merrill Lynch because Mike Tyson's account executive had refused to turn over financial records to Robin Givens without his customer's authorization. Givens returned to Japan a week before the fight followed by Don King who already was taking steps to move the Givens-Roper team into his corner.

At that moment what really was troubling Mike Tyson was the absence of Jim Jacobs who was lying in a bed in Mount Sinai Hospital in New York City. Jacobs had been battling leukemia for a number of years, and things weren't looking good for him. Before Cus D'Amato died, he told his adopted son that he should look to Jim Jacobs as the person whom he could most trust in his absence. After D'Amato died on November 4, 1985, Jim Jacobs assumed the role of father figure, spending a great deal of time with Tyson as counselor and best friend.

When Mike Tyson finally got in the ring with Tony Tubbs, these unhappy circumstances didn't distract him. The undisputed heavyweight champion, as he already had done so many times, made short work of his opponent. He wanted to perform better than ever to get the fight over with quickly so he could attend to other pressing matters. Tyson knocked out Tubbs in the second round. The two people closest to him were suffering, and he needed to give them his undivided attention. Givens was having stomach pains and began vomiting, most likely related to complications from her pregnancy. And Tyson was eager to return to New York so that he could visit Jim Jacobs who remained hospitalized.

Among the passengers on the Japan Airlines flight back to New York were Camille Ewald, Givens and Roper, trainers Kevin Rooney and Steve Lott, and co-manager Bill Cayton and his cardiologist. Even Don King was on board that flight, exercising his trademark, non-stop blabber on anybody willing to listen to him.

During the flight Bill Cayton and Steve Lott discussed plans for the upcoming match with Michael Spinks scheduled for June 27 at Convention Hall in Atlantic City. The fight had been receiving a great deal of publicity. Spinks won a gold medal in the 1976 Olympics, and he was undefeated in thirty-one professional fights. Not long into the flight Robin Givens approached Cayton and demanded he comply with her request to turn over papers relating to the management of her husband. He assured her that she would get those documents as soon as he returned to his office.

I sat back and tried to get some sleep on the long flight across the Pacific Ocean. One thing was crystal clear: 1988 was going to be a very different type of year. The Tyson Tradition that Cus D'Amato started in 1979 was in for some very rocky times. There were some new kids on the block named Robin Givens and Ruth Roper. And with Don King waiting in the wings and adding more fuel to the fire, there was no doubt there would be a tremendous amount of heat in the days to come.

***

Jim Jacobs died on March 23, 1988, the day after we landed at JFK on our return trip from the Tyson-Tubbs fight in Japan. We flew out to California to attend his funeral in Culver City. At the service the rabbi recalled the very interesting life of Mike Tyson's co-manager. Jim Jacobs had been a championship handball player, a light-heavyweight boxer, a master collector of baseball cards and professional boxing films, and a financial wizard. My boss, was one of the pallbearers and cried throughout the ordeal. Jim Jacobs' death hit Mike Tyson harder than any boxing opponent could ever dream.

Robin Givens and her mother had no interest in attending the funeral of this very important figure in Mike

Tyson's life. Instead, they decided to return to the offices of Merrill Lynch and make demands on Jim Brady, MT's account executive. They had anticipated that things would be different this time: Givens had a document turning over control of Tyson's financial accounts to her. There were angry shouts and accusations. When Givens and Roper weren't able to obtain the results they were expecting, they threatened to close the Tyson accounts and stormed out.

When we returned from the funeral in California, my boss wasn't interested in getting involved in the rivalries which had sprung up after his marriage to Robin Givens. Still crushed by Jim Jacobs' death, he diverted his attention to his newly-acquired home in Bernardsville, New Jersey. He was very excited about getting the place ready for the arrival of the couple's first baby.

Mike Tyson tried hard to demonstrate his love for his wife, leaving gifts for her, like jewelry under her pillow and roses on the night stand. One time he brought her breakfast in bed after hiding a large diamond in the omelette. Tyson was trying to do the right thing to make their marriage work. But Givens never seemed satisfied, instead acting like she was owed these lavish possessions, including the four-million-dollar Bernardsville Mansion. She treated MT like a dumb guy and failed to acknowledge his romantic efforts with even a kind word. Her attitude was more like: "Is this all you're giving me?"

I would drive Robin Givens to designer boutiques such as Versace, Chanel, and Gucci. She also could spend hours at Bloomingdale's. If Givens saw something in a store window which caught her attention, I would have to pull over. She would run inside and buy the item without thinking twice regardless of the cost. That's why I silently began calling her "Robin Gotta-Have-It-Givens." After their divorce, when I told my boss about the unofficial name I had given her, Mike Tyson had a good laugh.

***

The Bernardsville Mansion was a forty-minute drive from midtown Manhattan. Whitney Houston was a next-door neighbor. The new Tyson residence had twenty-five bedrooms and fourteen bathrooms spread among its three floors. Robin Givens took it upon herself to replace the original decor styled by the Vanderbilt family. She spent more money in renovations than the purchase price of the Bernardsville Mansion. The main staircase and bannister were ripped out and redone in gold at a cost of around one-million. The master bedroom had gold-leaf trimmings. Its bathroom had wet and dry saunas and a shower with twenty jets set at different angles. That bathroom was so big it accommodated a whole set of cast-iron furniture. The new Mrs. Tyson also ordered a Roman-style marble tub, designed by Gianni Versace and encrusted with diamonds, with a price tag of two-million dollars.

At the same time these renovations were underway, I was taking my boss and his wife to Brownsville so she could get to know his roots. Tyson would have me stop at soul-food restaurants and Church's Fried Chicken. Robin Givens wasn't particularly thrilled with these excursions back to the old neighborhood to see the "home boys." Givens didn't like being reminded about her husband's very humble roots. This situation eventually would blow up into a major conflagration in the not-too-distant future.

When the Bernardsville Mansion was finished, the

ten-pack Rolls Royce Silver Spur limousine was delivered. We had been using the grey fourteen-pack Mercedes with the raspberry interior. Now we had a Rolls just like in the old days when I chauffeured Tyson around for Michelle's. One thing I did at the time was to have a bag crafted so that we could keep track of the keys to all the vehicles in our inventory which now numbered twenty-five.

Robin Givens immediately took over as boss of the Bernardsville Mansion staff. Her quick temper and zero tolerance terrorized everybody. One time she told the chef to clean his jacket after she noticed it had a tomato-sauce stain. He was busy cooking so he didn't do anything about it right away. Later, when Givens saw that the chef hadn't followed her orders, she snapped: "Don't clean the jacket. Just take it off. You're fired!"

Robin Givens fired a lot of people who worked at the Bernardsville Mansion. Tyson would try and hire some of them back, but many refused to return because Givens was an abusive employer. It wasn't long before there were signs of a storm on the horizon for this marriage. Givens still had her television career and also was making films. This meant that she had to attend a lot of social events. Her professional commitments required that she be separated from my boss for extended periods some 3,000 miles away. When Givens returned to Bernardsville, MT would want to know everything that she had been doing while on the West Coast. When they attended social events together, Given would appear too friendly with other men. Tyson would fly into jealous rages, demanding to know why she behaved that way. Later, however, he would start feeling guilty because he had been fooling around while Givens was away. MT still was seeing Naomi Campbell and Suzette Charles on the side.

Although Robin Givens' belly did not appear to expand during the spring of 1988, in June she reportedly suffered a miscarriage. As his marriage entered its fourth month, Tyson restructured my duties, now "assigning" me to his wife. He wanted to know where Givens was, and what she was doing, at all times he wasn't with her. For example, if she went shopping, he wanted to know if she was buying anything for a man. MT constantly would beep me, asking me what was going on. Robin Givens didn't like the idea I was serving as her husband's eyes whenever she was out of his sight. The feeling was mutual.

It was around this time that two individuals, Rory Holloway and John Horne, began stoking the fires of discord between the young couple. Holloway was a Tyson childhood friend from Brownsville who had moved to Albany. He started hanging around MT all the time after his boxing career took off. Horne, who lived in California, knew Holloway from Albany. In the spring of 1988, Horne was able to wedge his way into Mike Tyson's life. The more Holloway and Horne whispered into his ear about his marriage, the more MT's jealous rages grew even though I hadn't collected any dirt on his wife. It must have been his old insecurities stirring up inside now that the reality of his marriage finally was sinking in. Robin Givens' spending sprees, the multi-million renovation of their home, the expensive clothing and jewelry, coupled with her manner of frequently talking down to him, must have made Mike Tyson conclude that Robin Givens was no different than all the other women: after his money not him. With this in mind, the thought that his wife flirted with other men while she was away must have been unbearable.

One night when the jealousy really was getting to him, MT told me to take him to Manhattan where he did the club scene, Bentley's, Nell's, and the Apollo Theater, guzzling down $400 bottles of champagne. He really didn't drink that much because he didn't hold his liquor well. However, that night he went on a bender and got plastered. Givens also had developed the habit of constantly beeping me to find out what her husband was doing. That night she beeped me dozens of times, but MT told me not to respond. Back at the Mansion, I helped MT inside as he laughed and giggled uncontrollably. Waiting for us at the top of the elegant gold spiral staircase was Robin Givens in her nightgown.

"I'm only gonna tell you this one time!" Givens shouted down at me. "You use the service entrance!"

Tyson looked over at me. "Who's she talking to?" Then he looked up at Givens. "Bitch, the only servant here is you."

My boss stumbled up the stairs. Givens slammed the bedroom door and locked it before he reached her.

"Get away from me!" I heard her shouting.

MT kicked down the door and passed out. He was no stranger to sleeping without the comfort of a bed. Since I began working for him, I never saw Mike Tyson sleep on one. He hated beds. I heard it went back to some kind of childhood trauma. The first night I met him, at JFK in late November of 1986, he was sleeping on a ledge in a fetal position. MT usually slept on the floor or, at best, half-on, half-off a couch. And he never had sex on a bed.

***

The pace of the dangerous fireworks between Mike

Tyson and Robin Givens began picking up at the half-way point of their marriage. Although their sex life seemed good, they had frequent arguments, sometimes ending with Tyson and Givens chasing each other down the New Jersey Turnpike. There was a lot of shoving and pushing, the majority of which Givens initiated. She didn't know when to stop with her mouth or hands. In the heat of battle, Robin Givens would lunge at my boss and start scratching him. I saw him do his best to hold back. There was a good deal of yelling and screaming which included Ruth Roper whose strategic location in an adjacent bedroom allowed her to know what was going on between the couple. Tyson didn't want Roper in the house, but Givens insisted, not only that her mother live with them, but also that she occupy a bedroom right next to theirs.

It wasn't long before there was another major clash between the couple which ended up being their biggest ever. My boss had planned a party for all his friends from the old Brownsville neighborhood. He wanted to give them the opportunity to have a good time for a full day away from the ghetto. He was expecting around two-hundred people to attend, and he hired a company to make barbecue. During the morning of the day of the party, a huge truck pulled up to the Bernardsville Mansion, and its crew went to work preparing the big feast.

As we waited for the guests to arrive, I was with MT and Anthony watching our boss's favorite videos, *Tom and Jerry* and *Roadrunner* cartoons and martial-arts movies. Robin Givens was notably absent, having taken off earlier in her silver-grey Porsche for a shopping excursion in the City where she would hit her favorite spots, Chanel, Gucci,

Versace and, of course, Bloomingdale's. We were advised that another big truck had pulled into the driveway. We went outside to find out what was going on because we weren't expecting any more deliveries.

The driver asked us where we wanted him to put the portable toilets. The problem was we hadn't ordered any. I noticed MT's facial muscles twitching with anger.

"Rudy, call that bitch up and ask her why we have this truck here."

I was able to reach Givens on her mobile phone. "Robin, the boss wanted me to ask if you ordered some portable toilets for the party." Givens preferred that I call her by her first name instead of "Mrs. Tyson."

"Yes, I ordered the toilets. I don't want any of those nasty niggers from Brooklyn using my bathrooms."

I turned to MT. "Yes, sir, she did order them. She said she doesn't want any of those nasty niggers using..."

"Tell her to get her ass home now!"

Mike Tyson was both embarrassed and angry that his wife didn't think his friends from the old neighborhood were good enough to use the bathrooms in their home. His wife had overstepped one boundary she could never cross no matter how much he was in love with her. Tyson never lost sight of who he was or where he came from. He ordered the portable toilets removed from the property. A little while later Robin Givens zoomed into the driveway and made her way to the tv room where we all were sitting.

"What's the problem?" she snapped.

Tyson jumped up and grabbed her by the neck. We also jumped up and pleaded with him to release her.

"Who are you to call my friends nasty niggers?" he

yelled, then kicked her in the ass. "Go to your room!"

Ruth Roper descended from the second floor and confronted Tyson. He was sick and tired of his mother-in-law constantly scolding him for his manners and behavior toward her daughter. A shouting match broke out.

"She thinks she's white. She's as black as anything around here!"

There was no way Tyson was going to apologize for his behavior. It was almost noon, and he turned to me.

"I need a favor, Rudy. I want you to make as many trips to Brooklyn as it takes. Pick up everybody. And, Rudy, treat everybody the same."

The humble folks back in Brownsville had one hell of a time. I made seven round trips that day, picking up Tyson's guests at the housing projects. They were being transported to the Bernardsville Mansion in a Rolls Royce limousine, their driver a very sharply-dressed young chauffeur who treated them like royalty. Tyson had spent a lot of money on my clothing. As far as I knew, I was the only chauffeur who dressed in leather and had alligator shoes. Mike Tyson believed that if his chauffeur looked like a million bucks, then he would look like a billion sitting in the back of the limousines I drove for him.

That day I remember picking up one guy, William Fagan, who looked like he had been working under a car for three weeks. He was very worried that he was going to mess up the limo, but I told him to get in. I stopped at a store and bought him a sweat suit and sneakers. I didn't know at the time that he was one of Tyson's closest childhood friends. Apparently, word got back to my boss about how well I had treated this particular guest. In fact, many told him I had been extremely polite and helpful to all of them. I didn't even know that one of the passengers was Tyson's aunt. She had a problem walking, and I had helped her down the stairs of her apartment building. One reason MT kept me in his service longer than anybody else was because I always made it a point to treat everybody professionally and courteously.

"Rudy, don't judge people because we're all the same," MT would say. "Don't let the money change you."

The party was a big success. After I had brought the last group of guests from his old neighborhood, MT walked over to me with a plate of chicken and ribs.

"Hey, take a break," he said, handing me the plate.

"You've been driving my people around all day. Let's have dinner together."

Tyson told me that everybody was bragging about how great his chauffeur had treated them. This was the first time my boss pulled me out of the role of chauffeur and personal assistant and consulted with me like a friend, leaving his guests to themselves for awhile.

After we had wolfed down the delicious barbecue, MT said: "That Robin. I can't believe she'd do this to me. I don't understand why she's so selfish and greedy. She doesn't want my people to use our toilets. Even if they broke them all, I've got enough money to rebuild them tomorrow."

Rather than pour fuel on the fire, I decided to throw water on it. "Robin is like that," I said, "because she's just trying to protect your investments. There's a lot of stuff that could get broken."

"She's more worried about my people stealing the diamonds from the tubs. Why did the bitch order those tubs anyway? She never takes a bath in them."

He waved his arm around showing the expanse of the estate. "Rudy, don't let this shit get to you. We're just regular people."

Back then it was easy to see that Mike Tyson cared about all types of people. The two who rescued him from an infamous juvenile reformatory and raised him as their own son, Cus D'Amato and Camille Ewald, were white. Jim Jacobs, his co-manager who took over as father figure after D'Amato died, was Jewish. And Tyson picked me, a Puerto Rican, to be his first and only full-time chauffeur and later personal assistant and bodyguard. Back then my boss had close friends of all races, ethnic groups, and religions. Mike Tyson couldn't be prejudiced because his experience had taught him that racism was, if anything, just plain wrong. However, things were about to happen which would take my boss down a very different and dangerous road. It soon would come to pass that Mike Tyson would turn his back on the life-changing experiences and long-term friendships which had pulled him from the ghetto and made him a world-champion boxer.

***

After the big barbecue party with Mike Tyson's old friends from Brooklyn, the couple's marriage really began to unravel. In September of 1988 Robin Givens was scheduled to go to Moscow for two weeks to shoot her television sitcom, *Head of the Class*. MT decided he should make that trip too. And, as she did most of the time, Givens' mother also would accompany her daughter.

Robin Givens filed for divorce a few weeks after returning from the Soviet Union. In the petition filed in Los

Angeles, Givens claimed that Mike Tyson had been out of control during that trip. She said he had thrown champagne bottles around their hotel room. She also stated that he drank glass after glass of vodka at the hotel bar, returned to their room, downed lithium pills, and then talked about committing suicide. After that he threatened to kill her and her mother and chased them down to the lobby. When a Russian police officer tried to intervene, Givens said that Tyson threatened him. She also claimed that her husband had "hung from the hotel balcony for about ten minutes, saying he was going to kill himself." Finally, she declared that Tyson had chased them around "from about 1 a.m. until about 5 a.m." and "only stopped because we had to catch a plane." All of these allegations were unadulterated bullshit.

"We had no incidents whatsoever while Mike Tyson was here," Anatoli Mikheyev told the media. He was the house detective at the Rossiya Hotel where the *Head of the Class* cast and crew stayed. "And if we had," he added, "I would have heard about them."

The truth was the couple had stayed at the Hilton Moscow where there was one incident. When Givens was a little too friendly with some men she encountered in the lobby, Tyson grabbed her harshly and shook her. In a loud voice he made known his feelings about her behavior, but that was the extent of any "violence." One of the co-creators and co-producers of the show, Michael Elias, said that Tyson had shown up on the set but acted "exemplary" at all times and "never raised his voice to anyone."

During the trip to the Soviet Union, Givens and her mother wanted to acquire expensive Russian furs. Tyson bought six coats while we were there, including a rare black sable which cost around $300,000. To pay for them, MT contacted Cayton and had him wire the funds, but Roper's appetite for furs wasn't yet satisfied. Just a few days after returning from the Soviet Union, Ruth Roper had MT buy her a golden sable coat with a price tag of more than $90,000.

The very same evening, Givens and Roper appeared on ABC's *20/20*. Robin Givens had told Tyson that Barbara Walters wanted to swing by the house and do an interview. She was kissing and smooching my boss, and he said: "Okay, whatever." Givens and Roper told Walters that Mike Tyson was a "sick, sick man," a violent manic-depressive, and that their life with this "beast was pure hell." Tyson also was on camera, sitting meekly near them as those two pummeled him with false and vicious accusations. This *20/20* episode was broadcast to millions across the nation. I learned later Camille Ewald and Jay Bright had watched it at The White House and were outraged by this humiliating spectacle.

Although Givens and Roper sent my boss to a psychiatrist who prescribed lithium for him, there really was nothing wrong with Mike Tyson. After Givens filed for divorce, MT was examined by a well-respected psychiatrist, Dr. Abraham L. Halpern, who was Chairman of the Department of Psychiatry at United Hospital in Port Chester, New York. Dr. Halpern performed a thorough examination of Mike Tyson and conducted background interviews of friends and family. The doctor concluded that Tyson was "free of any signs of psychotic thinking or behavior." Dr. Halpern stated that my boss did not suffer from manic-depressive psychosis or illness presently or in the past. The doctor confirmed his findings with those of Dr. Henry L. McCurtis of Harlem Hospital, the psychiatrist to whom

Given and Roper had sent Tyson. Dr. McCurtis agreed that Tyson didn't suffer from manic depression, psychosis, or any other type of major mental illness. He had prescribed lithium for Tyson only to temporarily stabilize his moods. Dr. McCurtis's diagnosis contradicted what Givens and Roper told millions of television viewers on *20/20* about Mike Tyson's mental health.

On October 7, 1988, a few days after the *20/20* broadcast, Marvin Mitchelson, the flamboyant palimony lawyer, announced he was representing Givens and had filed divorce papers in Los Angeles. Because California was a community-property state, Givens could sue for one-half of everything that her husband had earned from the moment they were married even though the marriage lasted only eight months. This was in contrast to divorce laws in other states, such as New York or New Jersey, where marriages were reviewed on a case-by-case basis to reach fair and equitable divisions of marital assets.

At this point Mike Tyson stopped using medications of any type. In a New Jersey court, Tyson filed a petition for annulment of his marriage or, alternatively, divorce, asserting that Robin Givens had tricked him into marrying her by making up a story about being pregnant. In an interview with the *Chicago Sun-Times*, Tyson said about Givens and Roper: "The issue is not money. It's just the idea that they played a scheme on me. They drew me in, they worked on my emotions because I was in love. They tried to separate me from my friends." In the California case, Tyson pled that he had "been tricked into marriage" and was "the hapless victim of intentional fraud."

I wasn't surprised by the torrent of false accusations

and humiliation raining down on my boss at the end of this marriage. Although not as easy to detect at the start of the relationship, as time passed it became clear to me that Givens and Roper didn't care at all about Tyson, just his money. For them the marriage was just one big business venture. Those two spent more hours discussing Tyson's financial situation than he did working out in the gym.

Muhammad Ali had several favorite phrases to describe how he had tricked his opponents into defeat. One of those was the "rope-a-dope." I thought how ironic it was that Mike Tyson's mother-in-law was named Ruth Roper. During his short and rocky relationship with Roper and her daughter, Tyson got "Roper-doped." He ended up settling the divorce litigation. After eight months as Mrs. Tyson, Robin Givens walked out of his life for good, millions richer in property and cash. On more than one occasion when he wasn't around, I had heard Roper and Givens refer to my boss's favorite dog, a bull mastiff, as "Mike Tyson."

"Bait & Switch"

"Bait and Switch"

After serving a four-year prison sentence in Ohio's Marion Correctional Institution for the murder of a business associate, Donald "Don" King, a numbers runner from Cleveland, began a new career as a professional boxing promoter. By the early 1980s, he was known as "the world's premier fight promoter." King had made tons of money during his rapid climb to the summit of this professional sport, representing world champions such as Muhammad Ali and Larry Holmes. However, by mid-1986, Don King began experiencing a run of very bad luck.

Don King's heavyweight fighters were being knocked out left and right by a young black boxer, a former juvenile delinquent from Brownsville with an eccentric past. This major new threat to Don King's dominance over the heavyweight class, Michael Gerard Tyson, had been living in the Catskills since age twelve with boxing legend Cus D'Amato and his companion, Camille Ewald. In fewer than eighteen months, that is, by mid-July of 1986, Mike Tyson had won all of his twenty-five professional fights, twenty-three by knockouts. And he was only twenty-years-old. The writing was on the wall: "Iron Mike" Tyson was going to be somebody's major meal ticket for years to come.

This stark reality became even clearer to Don King at the time he was arranging "The Heavyweight Unification Tournament" with Butch Lewis, another fight promoter.

King dubbed himself and Lewis "The Dynamic Duo." The Tournament was being co-promoted by the Las Vegas Hilton and HBO, and its objective was to crown a single heavyweight champion of the world. At that time there was no "undisputed" world champion because there were three major boxing organizations, WBC, WBA, and IBF, and each of them sponsored professional matches. The project was not going well for "The Dynamic Duo," advance sales of the main fight between Michael Spinks and Norwegian Steffen Tangstad so minimal as to spell financial disaster for the much-hyped "Heavyweight Unification Tournament."

To the surprise of many, Don King agreed to add to the Tournament the fight between Mike Tyson and Alfonso Ratliff scheduled for September 6, 1986. King did this very reluctantly because his cut wasn't going to be very favorable, only a fixed fee rather than his customary promoter's percentage. But he was desperate, and his strategy ended up saving the Tournament with sales immediately skyrocketing once it was announced that Mike Tyson was going to participate in it. MT's opponents along the Tournament's path, Alfonso Ratliff, Trevor Berbick, "Bonecrusher" Smith, and Pinklon Thomas, all were controlled by Don King or through his son, Carl. Each of their fighters fell like dominos under Tyson's crushing blows. At that moment Don King decided that he would do whatever was necessary to take over Mike Tyson's boxing career. Technology rapidly was transforming the entertainment world. Now there was cable television, and "pay-per-view" was just over the horizon. There were tens of millions of dollars to be made by whoever controlled this young heavyweight champion. And for Don King to retain his title as "the world's premier fight promoter," he needed to have "Iron Mike" in his stable.

Convincing Mike Tyson to jump ship and move over to him was not going to be an easy task for Don King. The Tyson Tradition was still firmly in place even after Cus D'Amato passed away on November 4, 1985. First, Tyson had a home at The White House in Catskill, New York where he lived with Camille Ewald and the rest of his adoptive family. Second, his professional boxing career and fast-growing wealth continued to be co-managed fairly and conservatively by long-time D'Amato intimate, Jim Jacobs, and his business partner, Bill Cayton. Third, the original crew, Kevin Rooney, Steve Lott, and Matt Baranski, continued to train Mike Tyson using Cus D'Amato's time-tested techniques. These were extremely strong forces and influences on Mike Tyson's life from which he could not easily be lured away. Don King knew that it would take extraordinary events and major upheavals in Tyson's life before he could hope to break The Tyson Tradition.

Don King got to work right away, checking the back door to see if it was open, even if only so slightly. As things got serious between Mike Tyson and Robin Givens, King realized that the way to get to the young fighter was through this tv sitcom actress. And because Robin Givens was in partnership with her mother, Ruth Roper, she too had to be part of the program. Don King began courting them and then started bombarding them with the party line: the white man still enslaved the black man, especially in the world of professional sports. It wasn't very long before Givens and Roper began chipping away at Mike Tyson's faith in those who had been at his side for years. They tried to convince Tyson that his white management team didn't have his best interests at heart, and that there were major discrepancies in his financial records. Their theme song, promoted by Don King with as much pomp and circumstance as he did with boxing, was simple: the white man has tricked you and violated your trust. He has been stealing your money. It's time to get rid of him and return to your people.

A few weeks after the couple married, Jim Jacobs died. The opposition was now minus its quarterback so Ruth Roper and Robin Givens stopped chipping and started hammering. They wanted Bill Cayton to fade into the background while they took over more and more of Mike Tyson's financial affairs. Meanwhile, Cayton was searching desperately for ways to fight them off.

Givens and Roper were working for Don King and didn't even realize it. They thought landing Mike Tyson would be for their exclusive use and benefit. But King was miles ahead of them. He was using Robin Givens and Ruth Roper as pawns in a very masterful game of chess.

Don King had been working various angles for some time in his quest to win over Mike Tyson's affections. There was the "hooplah" angle when, on August 1, 1987, after Tyson won his final bout against Tony Tucker in the Heavyweight Unification Tournament, King organized a "coronation" ceremony. Tyson wore a chinchilla robe, a jeweled crown, which King described as studded with "baubles, rubies, and fabulous doodads," and was handed a jeweled scepter. Tyson had not been impressed and, in fact, had resisted attending the silly spectacle. And there had been the "caring and concern" angle, when Don King flew to California to console Tyson at Jim Jacob's funeral.

Don King was very smart and possessed the special

talent of being able to see the "big picture." To increase the possibility of winning Mike Tyson over to his side of the table, King didn't want to be the one trying to sever the strong bonds between MT and his diverse, extended family. Instead, King left that risky task to his unwitting "dynamic duo," Robin Givens and Ruth Roper.

***

There was one obstacle which Don King did not anticipate as the Tyson-Givens marriage traveled down its rocky but still intact road into mid-1988. Something very big which had been looming in the wings was coming into the picture. Atlantic City was booming, and its larger-than-life star was a developer from New York City known as "The Donald." The Taj Mahal, the world's largest casino with 120,000 square feet of gaming space, was the crown jewel of Donald J. Trump's real-estate empire.

Trump had been involved with HBO for some time putting together professional boxing matches in Atlantic City. Several of them had Mike Tyson on the heavyweight card. He fought Tyrell Biggs on October 16, 1987. Tyson faced Larry Holmes on January 22, 1988. Tyson beat those two with technical knockouts. On June 27, 1988, Tyson went up against Michael Spinks and knocked him out after only one minute and thirty-one seconds.

The very high-profile, powerful Donald J. Trump was getting too involved in the world of professional boxing for Don King's taste. It was a world in which Mike Tyson was the biggest game in town. Robin Givens had connected her husband with the Trumps. She had been palling around for awhile with Ivana, The Donald's wife. The Trumps had become very chummy with the Tysons, eventually inviting them to spend an extended period of time on the *Trump Princess*, their 282-foot mega-yacht.

Don King began searching for the right wrench to throw into that very troublesome Trump-Tyson friendship. Because he always saw "the big picture," Don King also was looking for a way to eventually dump Givens and her mother. And what better weapon to employ for these tasks than the services of Mike Tyson's closest friends. Don King found those friends in Rory Holloway and John Horne.

Bill Cayton had been keeping a wary eye on Rory Holloway for some time. MT's trainers and co-managers made it clear to me from the beginning that they believed Holloway was a bad influence and direct threat to Tyson's career. They were aware Holloway took Tyson out for late night forays into the club scene. They also knew Holloway ran with a bad crowd back in Albany. There wasn't much I could do except to try and keep my boss out of trouble.

Tyson enjoyed taking trips to visit Rory Holloway in Albany, and I drove him there several dozen times during the first two years I worked for him. When life's stresses got to him, MT liked to hit the road to upstate New York. Although his parents owned a small grocery store, Holloway wasn't doing much of anything when I met him. Tyson helped his friend out financially with a weekly "paycheck." With this regular income and by living with his parents, Holloway drove a nice car and sported a Rolex watch. And in the very near future, another source of funds would make Rory Holloway an overnight millionaire.

Just like with Robin Givens, I didn't get along very well with Rory Holloway. In May of 1988, Tyson wanted to fly out to Los Angeles to track down his wife. She was supposed to have returned to Bernardsville two days earlier after shooting several episodes of *Head of the Class*. The studio hadn't been able to locate her, and my boss was furious. Holloway happened to be in LA at the time and wanted to hook up with Tyson. I drove them around in a limo we rented at the airport. At one point Rory suggested that we go to a particular comedy club. When we arrived, MT told me to park the limo and join them inside.

"Don't let that nigger come with us," Holloway protested loudly. "What're you still doing with that stringy-haired motherfucker anyway? With all the niggers out there without a job, why you keep hanging around with that fool?"

"Rory, don't tell me what to do!" MT was pissed. "Rudy's been with me for a long time. Leave him alone."

As I always did, inside the club I stood near my boss, keeping an eye on things so he wouldn't be hassled. A tall, skinny black guy named John Horne came on stage to perform. He reminded me of Jimmie Walker from the tv sitcom *Good Times*. But, unlike that famous comedian, Horne wasn't funny. Holloway had known John Horne from Albany before he moved to California.

After his performance, Horne suddenly "realized" Holloway was at a table with Mike Tyson and hurried over. Although he appeared "surprised" to run into his old friend at the club, it was very likely John Horne knew we would be showing up there.

"Hey, man!" Horne exclaimed, slapping Holloway's back. "What're you doing with Mike Tyson?!"

While he made small talk with Holloway, I could see the dollar signs flashing in Horne's eyes. He kept looking over at Tyson's gold jewelry and diamond Rolex. MT finally was able to locate Givens, and we headed for a restaurant where she was waiting for him. Everything turned out very lovey-dovey that night between MT and his wife.

Tyson wanted to drive Givens all the way back to New Jersey. He had a black Ferrari Testarossa which had been sitting in a Los Angeles parking lot for months. As a married man, his life now centralized in Bernardsville, MT wanted to bring all his important possessions to the Estate. Givens didn't like the idea of a long drive so my boss told me to take this beautiful, exotic Testarossa back to New Jersey. There were a lot of curious and envious stares on I-70 and wherever I stopped on this cross-country trip.

One morning, not long after the return from that trip to the West Coast, Tyson was eating his daily bowl of Cap'n Crunch without milk. The chef could be whipping up a delicious shrimp or lobster omelette, but MT wouldn't even look at anything else until he first had a bowl of what he called "CK." Tyson told me that he would be driving into the City with Givens for the day and instructed me to hang out at the Estate. Soon after they departed, I got a page from Rory Holloway to call him.

"Yo, Rudy, I need you to do me a personal favor. I want you to pick up a friend of mine at Kennedy and bring him to my place."

"Yeah, who is it?"

Holloway told me it was John Horne, and I thought to myself, "Oh, yeah, the comedian who's not funny." My boss would have wanted me to accommodate his close friend so I agreed, leaving a note for MT about where I had gone. I pulled up to the curb where Horne was waiting for me at the airport. When he saw the $400,000 limousine I was driving, Horne's eyes bugged out. John Horne literally was sniffing the rich leather seats during the drive to Albany. Four hours later we pulled into the driveway of Holloway's house, and Rory came out to greet us.

"Don't leave, Rudy. Give me a few minutes."

I was feeling a little anxious waiting around for these two after the long drive to Albany because it was going to take me another four hours to return to New Jersey. MT could reach me anytime through my Skypager, but I didn't like the idea of being pulled away from my regular duties. Finally, Holloway and Horne emerged from the house and jumped into the back of the limousine.

"Take us to New York," Holloway instructed me. "32 East 69th Street in Manhattan. And step on it. I need to get there fast."

I wasn't very happy about being told to make this additional trip, delaying further my return to Bernardsville.

"This is two tons of very expensive steel, Rory. I'll do my best."

"Just step on it, Rudy," Holloway said coldly.

Mike Tyson wanted to avoid the hassle of reaching for buttons so he had installed a voice-activated intercom in this sound-proofed limo. My two passengers didn't know about this system so I decided to get some revenge by eavesdropping on them. They kept babbling excitedly about their upcoming meeting in the City, but I couldn't figure out what it was about. They kept repeating that they "had to make it work."

Our destination in Manhattan, 32 East 69th Street, turned out to be a beautiful brownstone with two huge flags in front, one of the Stars and Stripes, the other a crown with the name "Don." I suddenly realized we had arrived at the offices of Don King Productions. Holloway told me to wait in the limo, and he and Horne disappeared inside the building. Within a few moments, a Rolls Royce sedan pulled up behind me. Don King, dressed in jeans and a leather jacket, got out. He was carrying a briefcase, his signature hair pointing to the heavens.

I waited there for three hours and watched the sun go down. I had tried several times to reach someone at the Estate, but there was no answer. Because it was only forty minutes away, although very upset, I was not as nervous as I had been during the long trip to Albany and back.

I'll never forget the wide grins which Holloway and Horne were wearing when they finally descended the steps of Don King Productions. They piled into the limousine, told me to take them back to Albany, and quickly raised the partition separating us. I was really pissed now because I was looking at another eight-hour round-trip before I would be back at Bernardsville. I considered clearing this additional trip with my boss. While I was thinking about what to do, I decided to again eavesdrop on my passengers by way of the voice-activated intercom.

"You believe that we just made the biggest deal in boxing history?!" John Horne was squealing like an excited pig. "We made it so fast and easy! Can you believe the nigger gave us one million in cash just to get the nigger to the table? I can't believe it! I can't believe it!"

Holloway lowered the partition. "Where's Mike?"

When I told Holloway that MT probably was back in Jersey after a day of shopping in the City with Givens, he ordered me to forget about Albany and take them straight to

Bernardsville. Holloway grabbed the phone in the back and began trying to reach Tyson at the Estate. We arrived just as Tyson and Givens were unloading a large number of bags and packages.

Holloway ran over to MT. "Mike, Mike, we did it, we did it!" he said excitedly. They started walking toward the limo, Holloway hugging him and whispering in his ear.

"Mike, Mike!" Horne started yelling, waving wildly at Tyson from inside the limousine.

John Horne didn't know Mike Tyson at all, but he was acting like my boss was an old friend.

"What are you looking at?" Horne asked me coldly when he noticed my expression.

"Nothing," I said. "What's the matter?"

John Horne raised the glass partition as Tyson and Holloway reached the limo.

"Why are you staying in the car?" MT asked me.

"Sir, there's somebody still inside."

"Who the fuck's in my limo?"

"It's John Horne, my boy from LA," Holloway beamed, shepherding MT into the back of the Rolls. "Take us to 221 East 62nd Street," he instructed me.

As the glass partition descended, I turned around to see what MT wanted me to do.

"Rudy, just drive the fucking car," Rory Holloway snapped and began raising the glass partition.

Because I didn't hear anything else, I started the limousine and pulled out of the Estate, heading back to Manhattan. I soon realized the voice-activated intercom had been turned off.

At 62nd Street between Second and Third Avenues, we

pulled up to a striking four-storey brownstone building with several security cameras. To my surprise, Don King opened the door. My passengers went inside while I waited for them to return. Around 10 p.m., while I was standing next to the Rolls Royce limo, a taxi pulled up behind me. Two men dressed in very elegant suits and armed with briefcases got out, climbed the stairs of the brownstone, and rang the bell. A few moments later Don King opened the door and ushered them inside.

I don't know why, but Don King glared down at me with a look that gave me the chills then slammed the door. I had a feeling at that moment there was something really wrong going on inside the brownstone. Four hours later my three passengers left King's residence, and we headed back to the Estate. After that night, and until near the end of the great tragedy which eventually was to befall Michael Gerard Tyson, Rory Holloway and John Horne stuck to him like he was their personal life-support equipment.

***

John Horne never returned to live in Los Angeles after that day I picked him up at Kennedy Airport. Horne and Holloway lived in an apartment near Tyson and also stayed with him from time to time at the Bernardsville Mansion. Whenever possible they would hang out with MT late into the night and then seek him out early the next morning. There was a very noticeable change in the nature of the conversations that I started hearing on a daily basis around the Mansion. It seemed like everything now was a racial issue. Horne and Holloway began pounding Mike Tyson continuously with a "black rap": the white man, Bill Cayton, was stealing his money; his white trainers, Rooney,

Lott, and Baranski, didn't treat him with the same respect they would give a white fighter; and they treated him like a child, keeping him on a very tight leash.

Horne and Holloway cranked up another "rap" to lay on MT designed to destroy his relationship with his tv actress wife. At the time it wasn't a certainty their marriage would fail. The Tysons had become close to Donald and Ivana Trump. MT valued their friendship, and the Tysons spent a good deal of time on the Trump mega-yacht, the *Trump Princess*. The more friends Tyson and Givens shared, the better chance their marriage would have to survive. So Horne and Holloway needed to convince Tyson that Robin Givens was taking his money while having sexual relations with others within the couple's circle of friends.

These two ruthless campaigns which Rory Holloway and John Horne were implementing represented very big gambles for them. There had been, and still were, many white people intimately involved in Tyson's life. Nobody had been more important to MT than Cus, except perhaps his own mother, Lorna, and his sister, Denise. Tyson also had great love for his adoptive mother, Camille Ewald, and great affection for his "brother" Jay Bright. Despite his skyrocketing fame and fortune, Mike Tyson never had turned his back on The White House. It was still his home, the attic bedroom his refuge, where he had spent countless hours studying Jim Jacobs' collection of boxing films.

Even though the training team was very strict, MT knew that Kevin Rooney, Steve Lott, and Matt Baranski cared deeply about his welfare. Mike Tyson had become very close to co-manager Jim Jacobs who had spent many hours counseling him after the death of Cus D'Amato.

Although he never had the same close relationship with his other co-manager, Bill Cayton, Tyson was grateful to both for their careful and conservative handling of his business and financial affairs. And Mike Tyson was still very much in love with Robin Givens, the girl of his dreams. She was someone he had thought to be far beyond his reach, but now she was permanently at his side.

It was a very risky gamble for John Horne and Rory Holloway to try and destroy these very solid relationships which defined Mike Tyson's daily existence. But there was a method to this madness. And it had been designed and patented by Don King. All Horne and Holloway had to do was set it in motion.

***

Rory Holloway and John Horne had taken over so much by the early summer that they now were ordering me to drive them around. At the same time, there was a new and frequent visitor to the Bernardsville Estate, Don King. Remaining co-manager Bill Cayton wasn't aware of this major transformation taking place in Mike Tyson's life.

Holloway and Horne used Givens' criticisms of Tyson's eating habits to their advantage, making fun of him for letting "the bitch" talk down to him. They also were aware that Givens enjoyed sumptuous meals the gourmet chef prepared for her while MT was stuck eating tasteless foods the trainers ordered for him while he was in training. Kevin Rooney worked closely with the chef, ensuring that Tyson's caloric intake was strictly monitored He usually was served very small portions of meat and vegetables, mostly turkey and carrots. It was no wonder Tyson wolfed down his food like an animal. He was always starving.

"Is this all you're getting?" I used to ask MT before I understood the training diet of a heavyweight fighter.

"I know. Can you fucking believe this, Rudy?"

That's why Tyson needed his Cap'n Crunch cereal every day. His trainers didn't bother him about it, and he consumed it dry to feel full.

One day, while Robin Givens was in Los Angeles filming *Head of the Class*, MT and I were driving around when he asked me to call Rory so they could catch a movie together. Holloway said he would meet my boss at Victor's Café, a Cuban restaurant in Manhattan. I waited outside while Holloway and Horne had lunch with him. I could see them through the window, and they were laughing a lot. After awhile they all came outside and piled into the limo.

"You know, that bitch is doing you wrong, MT," Rory said. "She's sleeping around. Why you need her?"

"But I love her."

I could hear Horne and Holloway giggling like two silly schoolgirls as they made fun of MT's response. They told him he was a fool, and that Givens was having wild sex outside their marriage because that was the reality of Hollywood. I had been noticing an evolution in Mike Tyson's attitude ever since Holloway and Horne had been sticking to him like Super Glue. He now was paying a lot more attention to their comments about Robin Givens. Once they knew they had his ear, their comments about her got increasingly vulgar. Tyson had assigned me to stay with Robin as much as possible, but I had never seen her flirting with anybody else or doing anything to raise my suspicions. As Holloway and Horne were well aware, if somebody tells you the same thing enough times, you're eventually going to believe it. It was a tactic used by all successful tyrants. Later I would learn that Don King was an enthusiastic student of Nazi history, particularly Joseph Goebbels' propaganda techniques. There could be little doubt that King was the real architect of these repetitive "raps" which John Horne and Rory Holloway utilized to change Mike Tyson's attitude toward his wife.

It wasn't long before Horne and Holloway pulled out all the stops to make Mike Tyson a single man again. They orchestrated things so that there always would be a lot of women hanging around whenever Robin Givens was out of town. And Ruth Roper was in the dark because she went everywhere with her daughter. There came a point in time when Tyson "groupies" were just about anywhere Holloway and Horne could get away with it, if not in Bernardsville, then at least in the privacy of the limousine. While Rory Holloway kept Tyson on a nostalgia trip back to their wild days in the Albany club scene, John Horne became responsible for organizing groupie sex.

During the final three months of their marriage, things rapidly went downhill for the Tysons. There were times when Givens called the Bernardsville Mansion from the set of *Head of the Class* and heard music blasting and girls screaming in the back ground. She would rant and rave to MT about his wild partying when she was out of town. After receiving so many megadoses of the "raps" Horne and Holloway laid on him, MT's response to Robin Givens became standard: "I don't give a shit. I'll do what I want."

***

By the end of the summer of 1988, instead of being a very big gamble, Don King's master game plan started looking like a sure thing. For several months two distinct forces had been hard at work to achieve one of King's goals, the elimination of The Tyson Tradition. First, Robin Givens and Ruth Roper had been wearing down MT with their "rap" about white people controlling his career and money. They already had been partially successful having secured certain concessions from Bill Cayton. Second, Holloway and Horne had been bombarding Tyson with a similar "rap" as well as others which included that Givens had to be cheating on MT when she was out in LA working on her tv show.

Not long after Robin Givens had humiliated her husband on *20/20* and announced that she was filing for divorce, Mike Tyson fired Kevin Rooney, the individual Cus D'Amato had selected to oversee his training. For years Rooney had worked tirelessly to take Tyson to the top of his profession. Rooney also had been a good friend to the young fighter along the way. In late November of 1988, my boss saw Rooney on television where the trainer gave the impression that having to deal with Don King was going to be worse for MT than dealing with Givens. The next day, Rooney, who didn't have a written contract, who had worked for years only on the strength of a handshake, was out. The second trainer, Steve Lott, had been fired sometime before. Now there was a battle between Cayton and King about who could promote Tyson fights. Don King didn't have any authority to do so, but that didn't stop him from just doing it anyway. The Tyson Tradition, a solid rock for many years, had hit the ground and broken into many pieces.

Mike Tyson never mentioned to me that he was going to fire Kevin Rooney or anybody else. Whether he made these decisions himself or just communicated what others told him to do, I really don't know. At this point in time MT's mind was so messed up by all the negative forces working around him that he just didn't want to know anything. For awhile he had been refusing to take calls from Rooney, Lott, and Cayton, the people upon whom he most needed to rely to protect his legal and financial interests. But Mike Tyson was too busy with his new life filled with all the intrigue Holloway and Horne provided. They had convinced MT his white intimates were doing him great harm. Almost overnight Mike Tyson was doing the exact opposite of what he had been doing when I first came aboard in May of 1987.

The numerous torpedoes Horne and Holloway fired over eight months were greatly responsible for sinking the Tyson marriage. But the truth is it really didn't take many. During the same period Robin Givens and Ruth Roper had sown the seeds of marital failure with their money-hungry attitude and their lack of respect for Mike Tyson. Another Don King goal was close at hand.

Emboldened by the way things were spinning out, Don King decided that he now could safely fire one of his own torpedoes. Before Robin Givens filed for divorce in LA, she and her mother returned to the Bernardsville Estate. At that time the Tysons were still close to the Trumps. "The Donald" invited the Tysons to spend an entire week aborad the *Trump Princess*. I drove them, along with Holloway and Horne, to Atlantic City where we spent time on both the yacht and at Tyson's Ocean Club penthouse.

One afternoon Robin went shopping alone while we stayed in the penthouse watching television. Holloway and Horne also were there. MT was wearing his favorite white t-shirt that said "Iron-Man Mike" which he wouldn't part with no mater how ratty it had gotten over the years. One of my jobs was to make sure that t-shirt was with us wherever we were traveling or training.

We got buzzed by security from downstairs that Don King had arrived and wanted to come up. Tyson said it was okay. King stated that he was going to have a big fight promotion in Atlantic City that month and wanted MT to get involved, including going to a press conference. But my boss wasn't interested because he was going to spend time hanging out with the Trumps. The two couples had planned to take the *Trump Princess* to the Bahamas for a few days. Don King was very upset that Mike Tyson was refusing to help him out.

"Goddammit, Mike, you've got to do this! There's millions of dollars involved!"

King needed a lot of hype for the upcoming event, and getting Mike Tyson in front of the cameras would ensure there was plenty of it. But Tyson held firm. He just wasn't interested because it wasn't one of his fights. King's demeanor and voice changed from irritation to rage.

"I'm tired of your shit with Trump!" King boomed. "Goddammit, Mike, while you're out with Trump on the boat, why don't you ask him why he's fucking your wife?!"

Don King stormed out of the penthouse apartment. Tyson had the remote control in his hand and threw it violently at the fifty-inch screen and broke it. I got scared because I had never seen my boss vent his anger like that except in the ring. The mere thought his wife was having sex with "The Donald" was unbearable for him. I went to the kitchen to get out of the way. Don King had blurted this thing out about Donald Trump and Robin Givens in a manner which sounded very believable. Tyson headed for the master bedroom and slammed the door shut. Fifteen minutes later, Givens sauntered into the penthouse carrying several bags from her shopping trip.

"Mike, I'm home!" she announced.

A few moments later I heard a big smack. As I raced out of the kitchen, I saw Givens on the ground and packages scattered all over the floor. Tyson had let fly an open-handed left to the cheek. He then stormed out of the apartment just as the maid came in. We tried to help Robin up, but she was dazed, her face still glowing from the smack. When she finally got to her feet, Givens went after MT, trying to catch up to him before he descended in the express elevator. Unable to reach him in time, she came back sobbing and very upset. I tried to explain what had happened, but she didn't want to hear from anybody. When Ruth Roper walked in, Givens screamed to her mother: "I'm not going to take it anymore! This is it!"

John Horne appeared and asked me if I knew where MT had gone.

"If I know him, he's heading for New York."

"Get the limo!" Horne ordered. "You're taking me and Don King to New York."

I got dressed and pulled the Rolls Royce limousine out of the garage to pick up my passengers. Just then, MT pulled up in the red Lamborghini Countach. I got out to see how he was doing.

"Where are you going with my limo?" he demanded to know. After I told him, he ordered me to return it to the garage. "You and me are going to the City in the Countach."

Tyson went back inside the Ocean Club to use the bathroom. I got behind the wheel of the Lamborghini and waited for him. Soon King and Horne appeared at the front entrance and started screaming at me because I didn't have the limo ready for them. At that moment MT returned from his trip to the bathroom.

"Don't you yell at him!" Tyson shouted, jabbing a finger in their direction. "Get your own fucking drivers!"

We left Don King and John Horne in front of the Ocean Club jumping up and down and yelling like a couple of spoiled brats who didn't get their way. We hit the street in the direction of the Jersey Turnpike. After a couple of minutes Tyson changed his mind and told me to head for the Bernardsville Estate instead of the City. He put on the headphones connected to his Walkman, closed his eyes, and listened to rap music the entire trip. After we reached the Mansion, MT raced upstairs and went on a terrible rampage, breaking furniture and smashing paintings. He also tore up a lot of Robin's clothes. I begged him to stop, but it was no use. I went downstairs and told the staff to leave our boss to himself. After about an hour I didn't hear anything so I went upstairs to assess the situation. Just like I had seen so many times before, MT was asleep, not on the bed, but leaning against it. I covered him up, and he slept through the night.

The next morning Robin Givens arrived and went upstairs. She had been accompanied to the Bernardsville Estate by Horne and Holloway.

"You work for Don King not MT," Holloway said.

Horne then added: "You shouldn't have left us in the street, motherfucker."

I tried my best to hide my intense dislike for these two assholes. "I'm confused," I said calmly. "I thought Bill Cayton is MT's manager."

Rory hesitated, then mumbled: "Yeah, whatever."

Tyson started tossing furniture out of one of the windows in the master bedroom. Givens called 911 and reported she was a victim of domestic violence. Several police officers showed up and began interviewing MT who by then had calmed down. There was no need to arrest Tyson so they left the premises. Givens descended the staircase carrying two bags and asked me to drive her to JFK. Horne then offered to take her there because he had to go to New York anyway. A few days later, on October 8, 1988, Robin Givens' attorney, Marvin Mitchelson, announced that divorce papers had been filed in a Los Angeles court.

***

A deceptive practice unscrupulous merchants use is to advertise a few items at very low prices to lure customers into their stores. When they arrive, the customers are told those items were sold out. Because the potential buyers already had incurred the time and expense of making the trip to the store, the merchants have a pretty good chance of getting them to buy something else more expensive. That scenario is the known as the classic "bait and switch."

Don King "baited" Givens and Roper into breaking up The Tyson Tradition. Those two believed they could take control of Tyson's skyrocketing career and fabulous wealth. King then utilized Holloway and Horne to pull off the "switch" and remove Givens and Roper from the equation. Don King, master chess player, must have had some good laughs as each of his pawns marched across the board. All that remained now for Don King was to make a final move, the checkmate which would give him total control over heavyweight champion of the world "Iron Mike" Tyson.

"The Kingdom of Darkness"

"The Kingdom Of Darkness"

Robin Givens left behind her a huge wake of doubt and insecurity for Mike Tyson when she stormed out of the Bernardsville Mansion never to return. Tyson's life would change forever after early October of 1988. The year had started off with such great promise for my boss. He had the girl of his dreams permanently at his side, and soon there would be a baby, making them a true family. By June, MT knew the joyful sounds of a newborn would not be filling their home. At the same time his dream girl was spending huge sums of his money, she began to openly disrespect him and his friends. To make matters even worse, King told Tyson in a convincing fashion that his wife had been "doing The Donald," a very rich and famous white guy whom MT believed he could trust. But soon there would be even much more darkness for Mike Tyson.

We collect many experiences over the years which make up our "life story." It begins at birth and ends with our final moments on this planet. Tyson's "life story" from his early years reveals a lot of unhappy experiences, doubts, and insecurities. There had been no father figure and little joy in his childhood home. By age eleven he had been sent away to the Tryon School, a tough reformatory for uncontrollable juvenile delinquents. He wasn't handsome or educated, and he had a high-pitched voice and a lisp. He was facing a life of crime, prison, and, very likely, premature death.

But as fate would have it, Mike Tyson's life story would take a radical turn. He would be rescued from the reformatory and taken into the home of two elderly white people who raised him as if he were their own son. His substitute father, Cus D'Amato, was a legendary boxing trainer who was convinced that, if Michael Gerard Tyson would just do things right, he would become a world champion. Cus D'Amato surrounded his adopted son with people dedicated to a common goal: the success of Mike Tyson, professional, financial, and personal. As the camera kept rolling into 1988, the script which Cus D'Amato had written was still being followed. So far the script had saved Tyson from a future filled with darkness and, instead, had made him a very famous and wealthy young man.

At the beginning of 1988, Tyson's story was turning into a blockbuster movie with a happy ending. But as Don King watched it, he wasn't seeing *It's A Wonderful Life* but rather *Nightmare On 69th Street*, the street where Don King Productions was located. Co-managed by Jim Jacobs and Bill Cayton, Tyson had been a thorn in DKP for almost two years, knocking out all of its fighters and capturing the unified heavyweight crown. Don King claimed to be the premier promoter in the world of professional boxing, a place where fabulous sums of money were made overnight. Therefore, not having control over Mike Tyson created an unbearable and unacceptable situation for Don King.

In 1988 Don King finally saw the opportunity to press the rewind button and then record over key portions of Mike Tyson's "life story." Through his manipulation of Robin Givens and Ruth Roper, and by using mercenaries John Horne and Rory Holloway, Don King was able to retitle and rewrite the script. This new screenplay was *Team Tyson*, replacing the previous title, *The Tyson Tradition*. The original cast, Cus D'Amato, Camille Ewald, Jay Bright, Jim Jacobs, Bill Cayton, Kevin Rooney, Steve Lott, and Matt Baranski, all were scheduled for elimination. The new cast, listed in order of importance were: Don King, Don King Productions, Don King's family, John Horne, and Rory Holloway. It wasn't going to be "lights, camera, action" at the filming of *Team Tyson*. There would be no "light" in this Don King production because the plot would revolve around a series of deceitful "raps" designed to keep Tyson in the dark about the most important things in his life.

After John Horne wedged his way into Tyson's life, he utilized Rory Holloway and his long-standing friendship with MT to convince him that "Daddy King" was going to be his savior. One thing Don King did was arrange for a very downcast and lonely Mike Tyson to be baptized in Cleveland at the Holy Trinity Baptist Church. The baptism took place on November 27, 1988, presided over by The Reverend Henry Payden and The Reverend Jesse Jackson, while Don King, Tyson's new "father figure," proudly looked on. A few days after that religious ceremony, Mike Tyson fired Kevin Rooney.

John Horne tried to convince Mike Tyson the white man was evil, telling him: "You're a nigger, and you've got to hang out with niggers." Horne's main rap was: "Let's rock the world because we're a bunch of bad-ass niggers who don't need the white man. We're not going to let the white man get away with enslaving us again." This strategy was classic *The World According To Don King*: if you repeat something enough times, then most people will believe it. In a *New York Daily News* article, former world heavyweight champion Larry Holmes said of Don King: "He treated me like a sucker, but I respect him for getting away with it. You know he's the best. He sells black. Don King is the black KKK, a black supremacist."

Horne and Holloway filled a huge, gaping hole in Mike Tyson's existence after Robin Givens packed up and left, his dream girl and dream life gone in a flash. He couldn't understand how the marriage could get so messed up so quickly. As a married man his social life had seemed more fulfilling. After the divorce, my boss often would walk around the Bernardsville Mansion by himself, dazed, confused, lonely, and vulnerable. His long-standing safety net, The Tyson Tradition, no longer existed. In such a weakened condition, much of the foolish Horne-Holloway "rap" started making sense to Mike Tyson. It was a perfect time to start rolling the cameras for the first scene of *Team Tyson*. Sadly, the plot did not include strict discipline or meticulous training. These things no longer were priorities and, in fact, would be excused by the end of 1988. The new people around Mike Tyson convinced him that there was no real threat to his heavyweight crown.

While King battled with Cayton for control of the fighter, Horne and Holloway plugged Tyson back into "the street" where crime and violence were glorified. They weren't just doing the regular club scene and staying out all night. Rather, they started getting Tyson to hang out with "gangsta rap" types in New York and Los Angeles. Horne and Holloway goaded Tyson into demonstrating just how "bad" he was wherever they went, resulting in a lot of negative press for their famous friend.

Once I almost got killed in an East LA club because I made a big mistake. Somebody had reached over and grabbed my boss by the neck. I shoved that guy away from MT and back into the crowd. Little did I know that he was a "Crip," a member of one of he most powerful LA gangs. That guy made a hand sign, the music suddenly stopped, and I knew I was in deep shit.

"Yo, Mike Tyson," the man called out. "Your boy wrong. He gonna pay now."

"He didn't know who you were, man," MT said.

It was decided then that I would have to go before the top Crip leader to see how the situation would be resolved. Outside the club there was a black kid no more than eighteen perched on the back of a brand-new Rolls Royce convertible sitting very low to the ground like a hot rod. As I slowly approached, accompanied by my boss and Anthony Pitts, I realized the kid was sitting down because he was paralyzed, a gold-plated wheelchair parked next to the Rolls. We found out later that he was considered the "czar" of all LA gangs. He asked what had happened.

"He put his hands on me," the Crip said.

The young czar exchanged words with Mike Tyson. It was obvious he had great respect for the famous boxer.

"This is my guy," my boss explained, nodding in my direction. "He's outta New York City, and he didn't know what's goin' on. He was just protecting me."

"I'm sorry, sir," I apologized. "I didn't know who he was. I don't understand the colors." I was referring to the Crip gang colors.

Finally, the young czar made his ruling. "The guy who touched Mike Tyson, he's gotta pay." He ordered the man to step forward so that he could be stomped.

Right in front of us that poor bastard had the shit kicked out of him by two huge guys. What I had done was wrong, but you didn't touch Mike Tyson. This was the court of justice of the streets, and this young paralyzed kid had acted as judge and jury.

Part of the plan Don King orchestrated was to distance Mike Tyson from long-standing friendships which had included people of all races, nationalities and religions. John Horne and Rory Holloway constantly were telling MT that his old friends "just wanted his money." Soon, King, Horne, and Holloway were convinced they had gotten Tyson just where they wanted him. If Mike Tyson could turn his back on Kevin Rooney, he could turn his back on anybody. Sadly, Tyson began pushing the elderly Camille Ewald, his substitute "mother," out of his life. He stopped making frequent visits to see her in Catskill as he always had done before. Those times we did return to The White House, MT would run up to Camille, give her a giant bear hug, sweep her off the ground, and swing her around. "Put me down Michael!" she would protest loudly. She already was in her eighties and easily could be broken into little pieces by her adopted son. But there was no hiding the fact that Camille Ewald truly loved this powerful show of affection. Camille acted like a little girl whenever she saw MT pulling into the long driveway of The White House.

After greeting Camille, Tyson would check up on his five dogs, including three "royal blood" Shar Peis. He didn't like small dogs, but these were Camille's favorites. After that, MT would walk over to the pigeon coop and take a look at the several hundred pigeons of all types he kept there.

Another ritual Tyson followed was to bring Camille some of the famous cheesecakes from Junior's, a landmark restaurant and bakery on Flatbush Avenue in Brooklyn. Camille used to fawn over MT around the clock whenever he spent time back in Catskill. If Tyson were laying on the couch, she would make sure he had a pillow under his head. Camille loved cooking for a big crowd. She also had a thing about making "real hot chocolate" using thick chocolate bars. Tyson never told Camille, but many times it gave my boss a very bad case of diarrhea.

Whenever we stayed at The White House, I would notice there was a daily routine. Camille and MT would disappear into the den which she had maintained exactly like Cus D'Amato had left it the day he died. They would close the door and speak privately for about an hour, not to be disturbed under any circumstances. They would talk about the advice Cus had given Tyson over the years. And she wanted to know about everything important going on in her son's life. Camille also would remind MT that she didn't like him driving fast. She found out he had gotten two tickets in one night and had to do community service hours, lecturing students at Catskill-area schools about the dangers of speeding. These same kids would see us driving around in a twelve-cylinder, 500 horsepower Lamborghini, giving us looks like "yeah, right."

"You're going to kill yourselves," Camille used to warn us. "Why don't you buy normal-looking cars?"

Tyson wanted Camille to learn how to drive so she wouldn't be so dependent on others. He told me to give her driving lessons, and she finally got her license. At that point, Tyson bought her a white Range Rover.

Camille Ewald had a talent for bringing out the true "son" in Mike Tyson. Even though he could have bought the local hotel, MT always stayed in his small attic bedroom where he had spent hundreds of hours watching fight films. A sheet tacked to the wall served as the screen. He studied history's greatest boxers, including Jack Dempsey, Rocky Marciano, Jack Johnson, and Joe Louis. Many of Tyson's techniques were gleaned from these films.

For a brief time after his divorce, and prior to his almost completely turning his back on her, Camille Ewald tried to help Mike Tyson heal from the tremendous hurt he was feeling. Because his self-confidence had been shaken badly as a result of his failed marriage to a beautiful actress, he began devoting his time exclusively to street girls from the hood. Horne and Holloway kept telling Tyson that Robin Givens and Donald Trump were out of his league, trying to convince him people like them never would treat him as their equal. I remember the time when MT had the chef hide a tennis bracelet, studded with very large diamonds, in an omelette Tyson served his wife in the master bedroom. Horne and Holloway got their "friend" into a mentality where romance only was for "pussies." Mike Tyson was on an emotional roller coaster, and he began acting very badly toward a lot of people about whom he used to care. He also started showing signs for the first time of losing interest in his boxing career.

***

My boss had been very fair to me from the first day I started working for him. It probably was because I acted professional, respectful, and courteous at all times. I always kept my distance, never pretending that I was part of MT's "inner-ring." If I had started calling him "Mike" at some point, Tyson most likely would have fired me. But after all this time had passed, I still was addressing him as "Sir." Meanwhile, Horne and Holloway continued to treat me like dirt. Those two tried everything to get Tyson to fire me, but it was one of the very few things they never could accomplish. This made them hate me even more. In fact, my boss kept assigning me additional responsibilities after Robin Givens was gone. He was depending on me more and more to keep his life organized. Mike Tyson trusted me because he knew I got results. I now was taking all of his phone calls, managing the staff, scheduling appointments and appearances, and giving him advice about his wardrobe.

Mike Tyson's next match was set for February 25, 1989 at the Las Vegas Hilton where he would face Great Britain's Frank Bruno. This fight revealed the big cracks in The Tyson Tradition. My boss's corner had new people. Trainers Rooney, Lott, and Baranski were gone, and Aaron Snowell now was the first trainer. It was obvious that it was not the same Mike Tyson who entered the ring that night. In the first round, Bruno connected with two hooks making MT stagger. Although Tyson won the fight with a technical knockout in the fifth round, his lack of effective training was taking its toll. His performance was noticeably sloppy. He didn't use his trademark techniques like rapid bobbing and weaving and swift combination strikes. And he appeared to be losing his patience and cunning.

When we returned to the East Coast, my boss didn't want to continue living at the Bernardsville Estate. In fact, he wanted to remove every item from the Mansion because they reminded him of his failed marriage. Tyson wanted to strip the Mansion bare, leaving it an empty shell, much like he saw his life at that time. Givens was notified and made arrangements to pick up a number of things. Whatever she left behind was sent to storage.

As Mike Tyson's chauffeur, waiting hours for him while he strolled aimlessly around the empty Mansion, I probably was the only person to know just how much he continued to deeply suffer. He always had been in love with Robin Givens and blamed himself for many of the problems leading to the end of their marriage. He was the undisputed heavyweight champion of the world. He was undefeated in thirty-six professional boxing matches. But Mike Tyson had lost the battle to keep his first marriage together.

***

The Ocean Club in Atlantic City again became our home base. Tyson wasn't training during this time. His next fight was set for July 21, 1989 at the Atlantic City Convention Hall where he would go up against Carl "The Truth" Williams. With Kevin Rooney out of the picture, no time was being spent polishing Tyson's techniques. My boss still would run in the morning, but there was nobody coaching him. Mike Tyson had become his own trainer.

What was getting a thorough workout during this period was Tyson's social life. With Horne and Holloway around all the time serving as cheerleaders, Tyson started partying around the clock. To avoid the risk of another deep wound, like the one he just had suffered with Givens, Tyson now was only looking for brief encounters with women instead of romantic relationships. The club scene provided a revolving door for sex, picking up women and doing the wild thing, gang-banging in the back of the limo, then dropping the girls off back at the clubs.

I soon realized John Horne never took advantage of the plentiful supply of young ladies passing through the rear of the limousine. However, MT's pal, Eddie Murphy, frequently would meet up with my boss to hit the club scene and participate in the sexual encounters in the back of the limo. I once risked asking Murphy for his autograph which I was going to give to my mother who really adored him. I should have known better because so far Eddie Murphy never even had acknowledged I existed. "Hey, don't bother me with that shit, man," he snapped, pushing the paper out of my hand. After that night I never again asked a celebrity for an autograph nor wanted to be photographed with one.

It was unclear whether Bill Cayton or Don King held official control over Mike Tyson's career as we headed into the summer of 1989. The Carl "The Truth" Williams fight was fast approaching. This was going to be Tyson's second and only other boxing match in 1989. But MT wasn't interested in getting involved in the dispute over who controlled his boxing career. At that point in time, he really didn't care what Cayton or King, or anyone else for that matter, was doing. Tyson only had one thing on his mind: taking on number one contender Evander "Real Deal" Holyfield. At the Tyson-Williams fight, both Cayton and King people were in my boss's corner. In the first round, after only a minute and a half, Mike Tyson was declared the winner, scoring a technical knockout.

After this last fight of 1989, my boss wanted a change. One thing he wanted to do was spend a lot of quiet time with old friends from Brownsville. I drove Tyson to visit one of them, Ouie, on Christmas Eve. After we arrived at Ouie's house, as usual, I remained outside with the limo. Tyson was so preoccupied with everything that had been going on around him, and so relieved to spend time with a close friend, he forgot I was outside awaiting further instructions. Hanging out with Ouie for several days, MT found a brief refuge from the darkness of "The Kingdom." They didn't talk about money or contracts or upcoming fights, and they didn't do the club scene. A large number of family and friends stopped by, and my boss enjoyed visiting with everybody and playing with the kids. Mike Tyson felt really comfortable in this environment, chilling out for the first time since I could remember.

For awhile we didn't hear anything from Don King or John Horne who were in Japan trying to promote a fight between Tyson and James "Buster" Douglas. On the third day of MT's stay at Ouie's house, Horne paged me. They had returned from Japan and wanted to speak with Tyson.

"Don King and John Horne are looking for you."

"I don't want to talk to them, Rudy. Say you don't know where I'm at."

After I relayed that message, Horne gave me the number for the mobile phone in Don King's limo. Horne later called Tyson's cellular phone. My boss handed me the phone, worried that King and Horne would track him down at Ouie's place. I told Horne we were on the Long Island Expressway near a certain exit sending him on a wild goose chase away from Ouie's house. But Tyson was still worried they eventually would show up.

"Shit, man, I've gotta get outta here."

As we sped along the Expressway back toward the City, Don King's limousine passed us, then dropped back.

A few seconds later, the phone rang.

"Goddammit, Rudy!" John Horne screamed. "You better stop that limo!"

"Don't stop, Rudy!" MT shouted. "Keep going!"

I accelerated rapidly, but King's limo, headlights annoyingly flashing behind us, was bearing down hard.

"What do I do, sir?"

"Lose them!"

I jumped onto an embankment and hung a u-turn, nearly flipping the limousine over. Now we were headed east back toward Long Island. I looked over and could see King's limo still heading west. Don King had his head stuck out of the window, his hair spiked straight up like a porcupine, shaking a fist angrily at me. The phone and my beeper went off at the same time. Tyson began laughing uncontrollably at this spectacle. I wondered what would have happened if I had wrecked this expensive automobile. After a dozen rings, MT finally answered the phone.

"What, Don? What? Fuck, no, I'm not going to Japan! I'm fighting Holyfield!"

Mike Tyson was going to fight Evander Holyfield, the number-one challenger, in Vancouver in two months. However, the James "Buster" Douglas fight Don King was promoting in Japan would make Don King Productions a huge pile of money. For MT, earning a few million more wasn't a priority. He already had great wealth. Instead, he wanted to fight and defeat the number-one contender as soon as possible because that's what a champion was supposed to do. Mike Tyson hung up on Don King.

"Don't answer the fucking phone no more. Take me to the apartment in the City."

As I waited in front of the Marlborough House on East 40th Street in Manhattan, I wondered how the rest of the night was going to turn out. It wasn't long before Don King's limo pulled up. King and Horne jumped out.

"You're fired!" Don King shouted at me. "And your games are over, motherfucker!" He turned to John Horne and instructed him: "Take the keys from the limo and throw that motherfucker out!"

I locked the doors before Horne could reach me. He started banging on the windows, screaming: "Open the fucking door, give me the fucking keys!" I just sat there listening to the radio and ignored him. He finally gave up and disappeared inside the building. After about two hours passed, Tyson, King, and Horne came outside. My boss got into the limousine.

"We're going to fucking Japan," he said. "So we've gotta get ready."

Mike Tyson had been transformed in this short time, suddenly becoming submissive to the wishes of Don King and John Horne. It was as if they held some special power over him which could take away his will to resist whatever they wanted him to do.

I drove MT back to the Bernardsville Estate where he wanted to pick up a few things, including luggage and a steamer trunk which had belonged to Robin Givens. He then told me to head to the Catskills for one of the few visits he would make to The White House after things started going bad. We stayed there for three days before making the return trip to the City. When we arrived, we went to Don King Productions on East 69th Street and once again entered The Kingdom of Darkness.

Having come down with a severe case of the flu running around the Catskills, I remained in the City while Team Tyson flew to Japan to participate in promotions and to train for the February 11, 1990 Buster Douglas fight at the Tokyo Dome. After I had dropped off everybody at the airport, I went to see my mother. It was the first time I really had spent any time with her since May of 1987 when I went to work full-time for Mike Tyson. Sometimes I would be only a few blocks away from her building in Spanish Harlem, but working for Tyson was a twenty-four-hour job. I never wanted to violate Mike Tyson's trust by doing personal things. I would call my mother a lot, always telling her: "Mom, I'll see you soon." My father had been released from prison and was back home. I was able to spend a couple of weeks with them both.

Tyson called from Tokyo and told me I could use his apartment at Marlborough House. I recovered from the flu very quickly, parked the limo in the garage, and pulled out the black Ferrari. My boss also owned a rare Lamborghini "jeep," originally built for the King of Saudi Arabia. It was made with 3/4" steel, was bullet-proof, and had room for four passengers and six bodyguards. It was designed to race over the desert at 200 miles-per-hour. Sometimes I would drive that "jeep" around the City if there was a lot of snow on the ground. It was such an exotic vehicle that one time it was loaned to the tv crew shooting an episode of *Miami Vice*. That down time in the City was my first vacation during the three years I had been working for Mike Tyson. By now I was a "celebrity" in my old neighborhood. I enjoyed being a "big shot" for a few days, cruising around the City in the black Ferrari with some of my old buddies.

***

Don King was milking the Japan trip for every penny he could get. Tyson's schedule was organized in a way to maximize how much money King could make. It did not matter that the hectic pace wasn't in the fighter's best career interests. There were rumors that Don King Productions was going to rake in $100 million in Japan. King had Tyson running all over that country. By the time I got there, my boss was exhausted. Everywhere MT and his crew went there were mobs of people taking pictures. Tyson was accustomed to locking himself inside the gym to prepare for a fight. This wasn't possible anymore now that Don King was in charge. Instead, MT's workouts in Japan had become public events. With all the curious onlookers everywhere my boss was training, I felt like we were in some kind of "freak show." We had been to Japan before, the Tony Tubbs fight in March of 1988. However, Tyson had trained in the States for that match and had only spent a short time in Tokyo prior to the fight. Now, Tyson was spending more than a month before the Buster Douglas fight doing endless promotions so that DKP could make a ton of money. As a consolation, whenever there was free time, Mike Tyson was banging geisha girls at the hotel.

Adding to my boss's problems was the matter of his diet. Tyson was having some very real issues with the local food, including frequent bouts of diarrhea and weight fluctuation. Our Japanese hosts always were very gracious and eager to please. However, we soon learned that if Tyson refused to eat local dishes offered to him during the numerous promotions, it would be considered an insult to the Japanese people. Once we were eating a particular dish and later found out it was rattlesnake. Tyson also ate some blowfish which made him very sick. Once when my boss requested fried rice, he was served beautifully-sculpted cubes but a very small quantity.

"We're gonna die of hunger," I used to say about the food situation in Japan. On this particular issue I didn't feel like keeping my mouth shut. We started checking out local American fast-food joints, like McDonald's, but the food there didn't taste like anything back home.

Unable to take it any longer, my boss finally said to me: "Man, get me Chef Early. I need some crunchy fried chicken, potatoes, and grits."

The next day the tall, distinguished-looking black chef arrived with a large supply of chicken, ribs, and steaks. MT was very happy to see his cook, the "James Brown of soul-food." He had hired Chef Early when his predecessor failed to cooperate about having enough Cap'n Crunch on hand so his first day on the job the new cook made sure to bring with him a huge supply. Tyson always used to say: "Where's my CK, man? Gotta have my CK." We fought over the prizes in the cereal boxes. Sometimes me and Anthony would steal those prizes before our boss got to the table, and he would hunt us down to get them back.

Chef Early wanted to use the facilities in our Tokyo hotel. This turned out to be an insult to the hotel's chefs and caused a big controversy. Consequently, negotiations were conducted, apologies duly tendered, and the Japanese conditionally surrendered. The kitchen was handed over to Chef Early as long as he agreed to teach the Japanese chefs the art of soul-food cuisine. This was necessary so they would be ready to better serve the famous fighter the next time he came to their country. We ate like kings once Chef Early got things going in the kitchen.

While in Japan, Mike Tyson learned about the health benefits of aged ginseng root. We went to a farm where high-quality product was available, and MT spent $5,000 for some very old ginseng root. Apparently, it made you burn calories faster, and it sure made Tyson sweat a lot. It also was supposed to detoxify the system. After he drank tea made from dissolving the root in boiling water, Tyson pissed black with a very funky odor. But he also felt very good afterwards. When we got back from Japan, MT continued to purchase aged ginseng root. He drank three cups of tea made from it on a daily basis.

It was getting close to the date he would meet James "Buster" Douglas at the Tokyo Dome, but Mike Tyson still hadn't gotten into real fight-training mode. So far his time in Japan had been invested mostly in promoting Don King Productions. King kept reassuring MT there was nothing to worry about, telling him that Buster Douglas was a "bum" who couldn't possibly beat the world champion. The odds-makers had the fight at a whopping 42-1.

Tyson kept insisting he should be fighting Evander Holyfield and wanted that to happen as soon as possible. However, Don King had to convince MT that Holyfield wasn't a real contender, the true reason being that Holyfield was controlled by rival promoter Dan Duva. As DKP kept revving up the jam-packed promotional pace, Tyson started shifting his interest away from the Douglas fight toward having more and more sex with beautiful Japanese women.

Whether on a level playing field Douglas would have been a real contender against Tyson will never be known.

Two days before the February 11, 1990 fight the field tilted sharply. That's when Buster Douglas's mother, Lula, passed away. And the mother of Douglas's young son had just learned that she had a life-threatening kidney disease. While Mike Tyson was cavorting around Japan for weeks with Don King, his image spread every day all over the tv and press, Buster Douglas, had been training back in the States. Now, as he prepared for the fight, Douglas was a very lonely man with a one-way-ticket to nowhere. Nobody even had cared to photograph the challenger at his weigh-in the day before the fight. Oscar De La Hoya had surprised the boxing world when he won a gold medal. He had promised his mother that he would place a gold medal around her tombstone. In the world of sports, a hungry man has an advantage over a man with a full stomach.

Unexpected things began happening right from the first bell. Buster Douglas started landing rights on Mike Tyson like nobody ever had witnessed before. At the end of the second round, Douglas hit Tyson with a hard uppercut to the chin. Tyson recovered ground in the third round with a big left body punch. Douglas wasn't shaken because he soon wobbled the champ with a chopping right, causing Tyson's left eye to begin swelling. In the eighth, Tyson landed one of his classic uppercuts which knocked Douglas to the canvas with six seconds left in the round. The referee, Octavio Meyran Sanchez, started counting two beats behind the knockdown timekeeper. Douglas kept his attention on the referee's hands, as he was supposed to do. He waited until the nine-count before getting up, and then the bell ended the round. This was going to result in one of the biggest controversies in boxing history.

In the next round, Buster Douglas pushed Tyson into the ropes and landed four big punches. Tyson was shaken, his head flopping backward, his left eye completely closing. At 1:22 into the tenth round, Douglas hit Tyson with a right uppercut, two more punches, then a chopping left hook which dispatched the champion to the floor. Never having been knocked down during his professional career, Mike Tyson stretched out his right glove and swept it along the canvas. Finding his mouthpiece, he was so dazed that he put it in backwards. Tyson struggled to his feet, and then he fell into Octavio Meyran Sanchez's arms. The fight at the Tokyo Dome was over.

This was a huge disaster for Don King. Suddenly, he no longer controlled the heavyweight champion of the world. This meant the eventual pay-per-view match with Evander Holyfield, worth an estimated $70 million, wasn't going to happen according to plan. Instead, the championship fight would be set up between Holyfield and Douglas. Don King had been too greedy, wanting to reap millions by promoting Tyson in Japan for weeks without training him properly, then putting him up against a non-contender. However, by doing this, King inadvertently had dethroned his famous heavyweight meal-ticket and bushwhacked his biggest payday yet. King had to launch a campaign right away to have the match nullified as a result of the referee's late eighth-round count against a floored Douglas. That effort failed, and James "Buster" Douglas officially was declared the new heavyweight champion of the world.

After the fight, Buster Douglas told a tv interviewer that he had won the fight "because of my mother, God bless her heart." The papers called the fight "the biggest upset in boxing history." *Time Magazine* declared "a story like this happens only in the movies. To be exact, it happens only in *Rocky* movies." Tyson's post-fight statement to the press simply was: "Greater fighters than I have lost."

Tyson's left eye was swollen the size of a baseball from the blows Buster Douglas had inflicted upon him. He was very concerned because several doctors mentioned he might have suffered permanent eye damage. It took a couple of weeks before it finally opened up enough so he could see. During that time, I had to hold my boss's hand wherever he walked. When we arrived back at Kennedy Airport, a swarm of media and sports writers was waiting for us. Mike Tyson had lost the heavyweight crown, and he desperately wanted to avoid everybody and head straight for the Catskills. Ten days later, MT learned that his sister, Denise, whom he loved very much, had suffered a heart attack and died. She was only twenty-four-years old. My boss was still in great pain from the beating he had received in the Douglas fight when we attended Denise's funeral in Brooklyn. It was only the second time I had seen Tyson with tears during the three years I had known him. After the funeral we returned to The White House where MT spent another four weeks quietly recuperating. As she always did, Camille gave him every ounce of her love and attention to help him through these tragedies. Many old friends stopped by to give Tyson their love and support. Fortunately, his eye completely healed.

Mike Tyson was very angry with Don King after the Japan fiasco. King never should never have subjected him to a hectic promotional tour lasting many weeks without any effective training for a championship fight. King had driven MT around for weeks like a fancy sports car, then parked him, leaving the lights on all night, the battery completely drained by the next morning. Meanwhile, Don King was starting to feel the full effect of his monumental blunder. The Mirage, a gorgeous Las Vegas hotel, decided to promote the next heavyweight championship fight, Douglas vs. Holyfield. This was the first time the venue also was acting as the promoter. To save a few bucks, and expecting a lackluster performance, Don King had signed Buster Douglas to only a one-fight deal. This was a big problem for King because now Douglas, instead of Tyson, was the "baddest guy on the planet." And just like what Douglas had done to Tyson at the Tokyo Dome, King had been knocked out of the Douglas-Holyfield fight before he knew what had hit him.

Things soon would turn from bad to worse for Don King. Holyfield knocked out Douglas in the third round of their October 25, 1990 fight at The Mirage. This win made Holyfield, the Duva-controlled fighter, "the baddest guy on the planet." Don King was a promoter unwilling to put on a professional fight unless he controlled both sides of the ring. King wanted it all. And to have it all, of course, you needed to control the champ. Years before, as his fighter Joe Frazier lay on the canvas, Don King bolted into the ring and stepped over Frazier's body, on his way to make a deal with George Foreman, the new champion. After the Douglas victory over Mike Tyson, George Foreman, now forty-one and on the rebound in the boxing world, chirped: "Humpty Dumpty sat on the wall, Humpty Dumpty had a great fall, all of Don King's horses, and all of Don King's men, couldn't put Humpty together again."

Don King knew it wasn't likely he would be able to

lure Evander Holyfield over to DKP from rival promoter Dan Duva and his company Main Events. He already had snatched many of their fighters, and they weren't about to let it happen again. But there was nobody else left in the DKP stable for Tyson to fight. Unless, of course, Tyson was hyped as a "great former heavyweight champion" who needed to fight other non-champs as he clawed his way back to the top. During such an interval there always was the chance Evander "The Real Deal" Holyfield would lose his heavyweight crown, thus permitting DKP to promote a championship match where it controlled both fighters.

One day at The White House we were watching an Evander Holyfield fight. After Holyfield won, there was a ringside interview where he was asked: "So, what's next?"

"I'm gonna fight Tyson," Holyfield replied. "He's a girl, and I'm 'Real Deal' Holyfield. And Tyson's not the baddest guy on the planet."

My boss's wild expression at that moment reminded me of Sylvester Stallone in *Rocky III* when, during pre-fight hype, opponent Clubber Lang, played by Mr. T, made insulting comments about Rocky's wife.

"I'm gonna fuck Holyfield up!" Tyson shouted at the top of his lungs.

You don't call "Iron Mike" Tyson a "girl" in front of anybody let alone millions of television viewers. From that day forward, only one thing was on MT's mind: kick Holyfield's ass really bad as soon as possible. And nothing was going to stop Mike Tyson from having his day with "The Real Deal" Holyfield. Or so I believed at the time.

***

Don King went to work right away on Mike Tyson so

that there would be no championship fight between him and Evander Holyfield whom DKP didn't control. King had repeatedly promised Tyson he would have his chance with Holyfield. But now King had to convince him that he first needed two "comeback" fights. It really was all about Don King buying time, desperately praying that Evander Holyfield would lose the heavyweight title while Tyson attended to other business. MT reluctantly agreed but kept wondering, if he was still ranked number one, then why shouldn't he be taking on Holyfield in the ring to prove it?

Mike Tyson's first fight on "The Road Back" was against Henry Tillman. It took place on June 16, 1990 in Las Vegas at Caesar's Palace and was broadcast on *HBO*. Don King had said about Tyson before the fight: "We just want to let you know he's alive and kicking." After the Buster Douglas upset, the media had been publishing numerous stories about Tyson's heavy drinking, fast cars, late-night clubbing, wild women, manic-depression, and an alleged suicide attempt.

Mike Tyson was interviewed before the Tillman fight and asked what went wrong in Japan which caused the Buster Douglas fiasco. "I made a big mistake. I didn't respect the championship at that particular time. I was in good shape physically, but emotionally I wasn't right. Basically, I screwed up. I'm no less of a fighter. I'm not on the verge of killing myself."

As the first bell sounded, Tyson bolted out of his corner and went on the attack. Henry Tillman landed a few punches to Tyson's body, but they looked and sounded like he was hitting a brick wall. At 2:47 into the first round, Tyson landed a lightning overhand right to Tillman's temple, knocking him out. Mike Tyson showed the critics that night he still could be a ferocious fighter. There was no question that Tyson was hungry after his embarrassing loss to Douglas at the Tokyo Dome four months before. "I fought the way I always fight," Tyson told the press. "I just fought with a little more appetite."

When Tillman went down, the first one to rush to his side was Tyson. "I just wanted to make sure he was okay," Tyson said. "We're friends. It just happens that we are good friends in the same business."

The only other fight for Mike Tyson for the balance of 1990 was another "Road to Recovery" match. It was against Alex "The Destroyer" Stewart on December 8 at Atlantic City's Convention Hall and also was broadcast on *HBO*. King had arranged an undercard light-welterweight title bout, Mexico's Julio Cesar Chavez against South Korea's Kyung-Duk Ahn. Chavez's record at the time was 72-0 with 59 knockouts.

Before the fight, Richie Giachetti, my boss's new trainer, responded to fight commentators who were saying that Mike Tyson's trademark "peek-a-boo" and "bobbing and weaving" techniques had been noticeably absent from the Henry Tillman bout.

"We haven't done anything to change Mike's style," Giachetti said. "It's just the natural evolution in a fighter."

Prior to December 8, 1990, the date of the Alex Stewart match, Tyson had gotten himself into better shape, now weighing in at 217 pounds. A few months before he had ballooned up to 230 pounds. Some people in the boxing business were saying that Tyson looked as good as when he had made short work of Michael Spinks, knocking him out in the first 91 seconds back on June 27, 1988 at the same Atlantic City Convention Hall.

Within eight seconds of the first bell, Tyson connected with a right to Stewart's head, bringing him to the floor. Alex "The Destroyer" Stewart went down once again with another right before the final, match-winning blow at 2:27 into the first round. Tyson had been so wound up to finish off his opponent that, fifty seconds into the fight, he fell on his stomach when he missed with one of his lightning jabs. By the time the fight ended, he had knocked Stewart down three times and had connected with twenty-one out of his forty-six swings. Alex Stewart swung out eighteen times but landed only four punches. After Tyson knocked Stewart to the canvas with the final blow, Don King rushed into the ring screaming "We're back! Watch our smoke now!" Tyson earned $2.5 million and Stewart $375,000. Julio Cesar Chavez also won his fight by a knockout at 2:14 into the third round.

"I just wanted to explode on him," Tyson told reporters. "I was hungry."

***

The Mirage, a gorgeous resort and casino on the Las Vegas strip, with 3,044 rooms and an exotic Polynesian theme, opened on November 22, 1989 under the dynamic leadership of developer Steve Wynn. The Mirage agreed to promote newly-crowned heavyweight champion James "Buster" Douglas in a title bout against Evander "The Real Deal" Holyfield. Suddenly, Don King had to come to terms with the fact there was a new kid on the block, a block which he desperately had been trying to control by erecting toll booths at each end. Now it looked like the new kid had slipped by without first paying the toll. Don King needed to have a heart-to-heart as soon as possible with Steve Wynn. Immediately after the Tyson-Stewart fight, King approached the Las Vegas developer with the idea of holding Tyson fights at The Mirage on an exclusive basis. Mike Tyson would fight nowhere else.

It was an opportune moment for King to make the overture. October 25, 1990, the Mirage-sponsored Buster Douglas performed miserably against Holyfield who now had become the undisputed heavyweight world champion. Holyfield was controlled by the Duvas and their company, Main Events, which had a relationship with another Las Vegas hotel. King's pitch to Steve Wynn was: "At a time like this, what you need is a promoter like me. I know the boxing game better than anyone else. The wave of the future for the really big bucks is going to be pay-per-view. Don't worry about *HBO* because I have something cooking with rival cable network *Showtime*. All you have to do is leave everything in my hands." Don King Productions had been negotiating a deal with *Showtime* executives who had embraced the idea with great enthusiasm. The proposal was to sell live Tyson fights on a pay-per-view basis for around $40, and then a week later broadcast reruns of the fights to regular *Showtime* subscribers.

Don King convinced a reluctant Mike Tyson to send a headline-making message to his fans: he was walking away from *HBO*, Donald J. Trump, and Atlantic City, destination *KingVision/Showtime*, Don King, and Las Vegas. This was happening even though Bill Cayton still was Mike Tyson's manager of record until early 1992 when his current contract would expire. Three days after the Alex Stewart fight was over we were on a plane to Las Vegas.

**

I never will forget that first day we approached The
Mirage. This resort and casino was a magnet, pulling you
inside where its luxurious interior consumed you. At the
entrance there were lagoons and a live volcano which every
few minutes erupted, spewing smoke and fire one hundred
feet into the sky. Its "White Tiger Habitat" was home to rare
tigers for the internationally-famous "Siegfried and Roy
Show." In the front lobby there was a 20,000 gallon
aquarium stocked with sharks, rays, and angelfish. The
Mirage made me feel very small as I strolled through it on the
way to Steve Wynn's executive offices.

In sharp contrast to the rest of the hotel and casino,
Mr. Wynn's office was modest and functional. A meeting
was in progress, but Steve Wynn ushered us in anyway and
enthusiastically shook our hands. He was a big Mike Tyson
fan and had been following his career for some time. Mr.
Wynn told MT how much he loved to watch him box. He
called in his secretary and told her to make arrangements for
us to stay in the VIP suite on the top floor next to where
Michael Jackson had a residence.

Steve Wynn's personal assistant gave us a grand tour
of the facilities. She got us security cards and keys to the
snack bar which was more like a well-stocked kitchen. She
also introduced us to the round-the-clock maid and butler
service for the VIP suites. We couldn't carry weapons in the
hotel but could check them at the VIP reception desk. The
personal assistant asked us if we had any special needs. I
mentioned my boss had several vehicles, including a
limousine, and we liked to park them in front of the buildings

where we stayed for easy access. She advised us that nobody was allowed to park in front of The Mirage. Even Mr. Wynn followed that rule. However, because he considered Mike Tyson a very special guest, Steve Wynn decided to make an exception for him. An area would be cordoned off in front of The Mirage where Team Tyson could park all its vehicles. So it wasn't long before we were displaying a brand new ten-pack Lincoln limousine, a black Lamborghini Diablo, a $750,000 Ferrari Koenig, a twelve-cylinder, six-speed BMW 850CSi, and two corvettes, one canary yellow, the other cherry red. Our parking area resembled an exotic-car dealership. A security guard was assigned just to watch over this very expensive collection. We were thankful for Mr. Wynn's attentions and returned the favor, providing him and his family with ring-side seats.

Because most people had to go through me before they could deal with my boss, I tried to be courteous and considerate toward everybody. If I acted like an asshole, they surely would believe Mike Tyson had to be one too. When people served us well, our philosophy was to acknowledge them with thanks and generosity. We always conducted ourselves in this manner at The Mirage, and soon the employees knew that we were the "good guys." The fact that MT was living at The Mirage generated a great deal of interest in the resort and casino. Thousands of visitors hoped to catch a glimpse of the world-famous heavyweight fighter. We sported beautiful Jeff Hamilton crafted Team Tyson leather jackets everywhere we went in Vegas, and we were easily recognized from a distance, people shouting out: "There go the Tyson guys!"

Everything seemed pretty much on track during

January and February of 1991, our first two months in Las Vegas. Mike Tyson was in better spirits after his decisive victories against Henry Tillman and Alex Stewart. Even though there still were legal battles going on about who controlled his career, as usual my boss stayed out of the fray. As long as the bills were being paid on time, and he had spending money, MT was content. Having been introduced to designer clothes by ex-girlfriend and super-model Naomi Campbell, Tyson continued to spend large sums of money on his wardrobe. He was buying almost exclusively at Gianni Versace, $2,700 shirts, $2,000 belts, $7,000 leather pants, and a leather bomber jacket for $78,000. Because I was in charge of buying his clothing, the sales clerks salivated whenever I showed up, making me feel like the Richard Gere character in *Pretty Woman*. MT would have me buy three of everything so he would have a complete wardrobe at each of his three residences, the Marlborough House in New York City, the penthouse on Wilshire Boulevard in Beverly Hills, and his sprawling estate in Southington, Ohio.

As we approached the March 18, 1991 fight against Donovan "Razor" Ruddock, Mike Tyson was determined to remain focused on his training regimen with Richie Giachetti, anticipating he finally would get his shot at the title with "The Real Deal" Holyfield very soon. And things also were going better for me as well because I had started dating several gorgeous young ladies who worked at The Mirage.

***

On March 18, 1991, in The Mirage's outdoor arena, the Tyson-Ruddock fight ended in a fashion nobody had anticipated except maybe Don King. In the first round, Tyson charged out at the well-muscled, 228-pound Jamaican.

"Razor" Ruddock survived Tyson's initial attack. In the next round, he went down for an eight-count, but that was only because he inadvertently hooked Tyson's leg causing him to fall. In the third round, Tyson connected with a hook after the big Jamaican fighter missed a right-hand swing. Dazed and confused, Ruddock hit the canvas and stayed down while referee Richard Steele counted out six. The bell rang as Ruddock sought the refuge of his corner, raising his arms to tell the crowd "I'm all right."

In the fifth and sixth rounds, Razor Ruddock landed a number of punches on Tyson, but they didn't seem to faze him. However, late into the sixth, Ruddock connected with two left hooks and a right one. Tyson moved in close and grabbed Ruddock who, breaking free, hit pay dirt with another right. Tyson was very upset and pointed to his chin, meaning "come on if you want some more." It wasn't smart to do that because Ruddock landed another right causing Tyson's head to snap back just as the bell sounded. Tyson later said that it felt like a "mule kick."

At the beginning of the seventh round, it was obvious Mike Tyson was very unhappy with his performance so far. He beckoned for Ruddock to come at him. Soon Tyson had landed two blows to the hips which, by their boos, many believed were too low. With only a minute left in the round, Tyson tried to make up for lost time and drilled Ruddock into the ropes. He combined with a body punch and hook to his opponent's head which caused it to snap back violently. With gloves raised, Ruddock staggered over to his corner. Tyson scored two more direct hits, a right and a left, again driving Ruddock into the ropes. Referee Richard Steele rushed in and grabbed Tyson with both arms. He seemed more concerned about preventing Tyson from finishing off Ruddock than whether the big Jamaican really was in danger. Suddenly, and unexpectedly, Steele waved his arms that the fight was over.

Donovan "Razor" Ruddock was shocked. "What?!" he yelled at the referee. This protest served as a battle cry for Ruddock's cornermen. Led by brother-manager Delroy Ruddock, they charged into the ring, including Ruddock's promoter, Murad Muhammad. Mike Tyson dealt with this spectacle by shouting: "That's bullshit! That's bullshit!" Trying to prevent any harm to the referee, Richie Giachetti lunged at Delroy Ruddock, telling him to "cool it." Murad Muhanmmad sucker-punched Giachetti, then kicked him four times after he hit the canvas. The bright-green jackets of The Mirage's security force began filling the ring, and Referee Richard Steele quickly was shepherded to safety. A few brawls still were going on in the ring, but the two fighters had retreated to their corners.

Richard Steele later declared that Ruddock had been unable to defend himself, leaving him with no choice but to stop the fight. "People just get out of hand because of the simple fact they don't understand boxing. They must come to see someone get hurt seriously or die."

Ruddock's promoter, Murad Muhammad, strongly disagreed. "All we want is justice," he told reporters after the chaos in the ring finally was over. Prior to the match, Muhammad had been uneasy about Richard Steele serving as referee due to his close ties to Don King. His concern was that, if his fighter started scoring against Tyson, then Steele would look for some way to eliminate Ruddock and hand the win over to an undeserving Tyson. Muhammad threatened legal action but later agreed that a rematch would be an acceptable alternative. Mike Tyson wasn't pleased either with the way things went down. He was convinced a few more seconds in the ring with Ruddock would have left no doubt that he had earned the victory.

The Tyson-Ruddock rematch solution to resolve this controversy was exactly what Don King wanted. If Tyson had scored a definitive victory against Ruddock, then King would have had to put up or shut up about getting Tyson his day with Holyfield. King couldn't let this happen because he still didn't control both ends of the street. Because the Duvas owned the rights to a Holyfield-Tyson fight, they would decide where the match would be held. This meant that the heavyweight championship fight would not take place at The Mirage.

In June of 1991, Dan Duva offered a record $51.1 million for a Tyson-Holyfield match, to be scheduled for October or November at Caesar's Palace, but that fight never was going to happen. Still Mike Tyson's manager on paper until February 12, 1992, Bill Cayton knew exactly what was going on.

"King uses Tyson's drawing power," Bill Cayton told *Sports Illustrated*, "to make these other fights and pays exorbitant prices to his stable of fighters like Chavez and Simon Brown."

Bill Cayton had in mind the $2.5 million paid for the Tyson-Ruddock undercard. King had his fighter, junior-welterweight Julio Cesar Chavez, sharing a sizeable portion of the purse at Mike Tyson's expense. Another Don King Productions undercard fighter, Simon Brown, received $1.5 million. *KingVision/Showtime* had revenues of around $28 million out of the $41 million gross. Don King's share was around $9 million after all expenses, including payments to each of his fighters. Tyson's take was supposed to be around $5.7 million. Had MT continued to follow the strategy originally mapped out by Cayton, Tyson would have been guaranteed $8.5 million for that fight as part of a deal with *HBO*. However, all that had been torpedoed by Don King when he enticed Mike Tyson away from *HBO* and over to *KingVision/Showtime*. When asked about Tyson-Ruddock II, Cayton said: "This Ruddock rematch just compounds the stupidity. Tyson should have fought for his title by now."

As time marched on during the rest of 1991, Mike Tyson began questioning more and more why he was wasting time fighting in other matches before having his long-awaited contest with Evander "The Real Deal" Holyfield. It made no difference to my boss whether there would be less money or whether the showdown were held at a Las Vegas hotel or in a dark alley. Mike Tyson wanted to fight Evander "The Real Deal" Holyfield *now* because that was what a champion was supposed to do. At one point the press got wind of Mike Tyson's increasingly aggressive attitude toward Don King, including a number of unconfirmed accounts that there had been physical confrontations between them. King refused a request by *Sports Illustrated* to either confirm or deny the rumors. However, King told *USA Today* that he and Tyson did argue: "When we do, I cuss him out and he cusses me out, and it ain't no boxing match. Ain't nobody screw with me, man. Part of my job as promoter and friend ain't to get my fanny whipped. I don't submit to that. I'm not afraid of Mike, and he's not afraid of me. We don't have to come to blows to resolve personal differences."

It wasn't long before a date would be set for Tyson-Ruddock II at The Mirage's outdoor arena. If I had been told that I wouldn't be around to see that fight, I wouldn't have believed it. But, then again, I had been wrong before.

"From the Darkness Comes a Whisper"

"From The Darkness Comes A Whisper"

We remained in Las Vegas for a few weeks after the first Tyson-Ruddock fight, hoping to get in some rest and relaxation. Don King also spent time there. He started the annoying habit of storming into our quarters, yelling "Goddammit, Mike, you're gonna watch something else besides those fucking cartoons!" It was at that time that we learned King had an extensive collection of documentary films about World War II and the Nazi movement. He would remove *Tom and Jerry* and *Roadrunner* cassettes from MT's video player and stick in videos of Adolf Hitler and the Nazis. Don King sent me to Las Vegas's main library to look for more films and even once had me fly all the way back to New York just to retrieve part of the video collection from his midtown Manhattan residence.

I remember a road trip in the spring of 1991 when I drove MT, Don King, and a reporter from Las Vegas to Los Angeles. King was all wound up in the back of the limo so I decided to eavesdrop by way of the voice-activated intercom. "The Jew was the nigger of Germany," King said, into his rap about how "Hitler did to the Jews what the white man does to the black man in America." What the Nazis did was to demonize Jews as "evil" and a "cancer which had to be removed." According to King, that's what "the system" in America did to black people by preaching "negrophobia," the notion that blacks were "worthless and shiftless."

Don King claimed the "the system" was responsible for him being "held back" by the white man, even though the journalist reminded him that he was the biggest name in boxing promotion and was about to close a business deal worth more than $100 million. King quickly changed the subject, going on and on for what seemed like an eternity about the racism against blacks in this country. According to King, the white man would never give the black man a fair chance to succeed in the United States of America. During this long drive, King had Tyson as his captive audience for this incredibly repetitive rap. Over time I had seen Don King utilizing this Nazi propaganda technique on my boss: selling belief through constant repetition.

The journalist finally was able to change the topic. He wanted King's response to numerous allegations over the years that he had stolen large sums of money from his fighters. Don King insisted that those allegations were just another example of white racism in America. Well-known fighters, like Muhammad Ali, Joe Frazier, Kenny Norton, and Roberto Duran, never had accused him of stealing their money. Only Larry Holmes had made such a claim, and King was upset the press had overlooked Holmes' retraction. King said he had done great things for Holmes who didn't have a penny to his name before meeting King.

***

In late April of 1991, about a month after the first Tyson-Ruddock fight, Mike Tyson decided that he wanted to "see America" by driving across the country in the black Lamborghini Diablo. He instructed bodyguard Anthony Pitts to fly back to New York, and then me and my boss headed east on I-10. I drove most of the way during the

3,000 mile journey while MT did most of the snoring. Wherever we went people recognized Mike Tyson, and he enjoyed meeting them, shaking their hands, and handing out autographs. My boss was no snob and never thought of himself as too good for anybody. Many fight fans were curious about the way the Ruddock fight had ended, and Tyson was very concerned about that controversy. What continued to bother him most was why he had to stand in line to have his day with "The Real Deal" Holyfield when there wasn't anybody else who should be ahead of him.

When we finally arrived in New York City, Tyson bought a new cobalt-blue Rolls Royce Silver Spur with a white interior and blue piping. We dropped off the Diablo for much-needed servicing. For a few days we toured the City, including a stop at Ultrasmith Systems on West 38th Street in Manhattan. Tyson had them outfit the Rolls with a 3,000-watt stereo system and headrest-mounted tvs like those on some airlines. The tvs were equipped with built-in Nintendo games which Tyson enjoyed playing as I drove him around the City. There also were stops at the movies, restaurants, and nightclubs. Mike Tyson kept going back to the same places and same lady friends. Based on recent events, it was better for him to know what to expect. We also frequently visited his old Brownsville neighborhood.

When we stopped off at restaurants, I wouldn't sit with Mike Tyson and his guests. Usually, I would have the next table over which I shared with bodyguard Anthony Pitts. However, if he was alone, our boss might invite us to join him. We made sure the servers knew his drinks had to be served in paper or plastic cups because MT had a tendency to break glass with his vice-like grip. We also didn't allow anybody to approach Tyson's table without going through us first. Anthony's massive build and, if he wanted, very menacing look, kept people at a respectful distance. Mike Tyson hired Pitts away from his bouncer job after he witnessed him pick up three guys at the same time and toss them out of an LA club.

Tyson decided to stay at the Marlborough House while waiting to begin his training for Tyson-Ruddock II. One night he entered my bedroom wearing lycra athletic shorts like the ones professional cyclists use. Because MT had such an unusually thick, muscular build, he could not wear regular underwear. He had been in his bedroom with a girlfriend eating Chinese food, but she had dozed off. He sat down on the floor and spread out a magazine.

"Rudy, I want to buy a bus. I want the baddest fucking bus. And I want it finished by the next Ruddock fight. Look into it for me, okay?"

The magazine was turned to a page showing a beautiful motor coach, but Tyson wanted something much bigger and better. He said he wanted to take another cross-country trip but with all the comforts of a luxury residence.

"After the next fight, if Don King doesn't give me fucking Holyfield, then I'm not fighting for him no more."

The next morning I called the publishers of the Robb Report, a magazine for the rich and famous. I needed to find out who made the best motor coaches in the world. Somebody at the magazine suggested that I reach out to Louis Normand, Jr. at Genesis Motorcoach International in Metaire, Louisiana. The type of vehicle Mike Tyson wanted never had been built. During my telephone conversation with Normand, I never revealed the name of the potential buyer. We made arrangements for Normand to fly to New York. I picked him up at LaGuardia Airport, and we drove to Pawtucket, Rhode Island where Hasbro, the famous toy company, had its headquarters. During the trip, I told him my boss was Mike Tyson and what he had in mind. He was very intrigued with the idea.

We sat down with four Hasbro designers and described the very special vehicle we wanted to build. In fewer than four hours, the Hasbro people produced a drawing of a futuristic Genesis motor coach custom-built for Mike Tyson. It had two bedrooms and a one-car garage, a complete luxury condominium on wheels. There was a lot of excitement as we admired what the Hasbro people had come up with in such a short time. Norman estimated the vehicle alone would cost $600,000. I was assured that everyone would work around the clock to finish the Genesis motor coach by the deadline.

The next step was to have Tyson review the Hasbro design and decide how he was going to furnish and equip the interior. We sat on the floor for hours while MT made his choices. There was going to be a lot of leather and marble and gold-plated fixtures, including a Roman-style tub. After we forwarded the final details to Genesis, we were told the final price was going to be $1.3 million. The company required an initial deposit of $1 million. That was fine with MT who ordered that fabrication of the vehicle commence immediately. He instructed me to call Joseph Maffia, the comptroller at Don King Productions, and have him cut the deposit check.

Because I was going to have to pick up the check anyway, I decided to wait to tell Maffia about this project when I got to DKP. After I explained the reason why MT needed the check, the people at DKP freaked out. Don King wasn't there, but he was alerted about my presence. King called in to find out what was going on. Everybody wanted to know who had put this crazy idea into MT's head. Maffia finally informed me that he could not comply with the request. If DKP issued a check for that amount, there wouldn't be sufficient funds to cover it. Maffia also asked me not to relay that fact to Tyson and do whatever I could to delay the Genesis project. I guess Joseph Mafia didn't know me very well. I worked for Mike Tyson not Don King or DKP. I didn't say anything, but there was no way I was going to participate in this scheme. I departed Don King Productions empty-handed.

When I returned to Marlborough House, MT was sitting on the floor, his back leaning against the sofa, like he did much of the time. He was eating Cap'n Crunch out of the box and watching *Tom and Jerry* cartoons.

"Hey, man, did you get the check for the bus?"

I related everything that had happened at Don King Productions, including Joe Maffia's request that I delay the project and cooperate in the deception.

"Call the fucking office! I wanna speak to that motherfucker personally."

Maffia must have told Tyson he would have to wait to get an answer from Don King. My boss was enraged, shouting angrily into the phone: "I want it now!" After a lot more yelling, MT finally agreed to wait a few days to pick up the check. That same evening Tyson had been looking at a real-estate publication and decided he wanted to purchase an apartment bigger than the one he had at Marlborough House.

He told me to set up a meeting with an agent from Brown Harris Stevens, the company listing Penthouse A in The Alfred, a luxury condo building on West 61st Street. It looked like the sale of that unit would be an $8 million cash deal. The lady agent agreed to meet us at DKP when we went there to get the Genesis check.

On May 2, 1991, around noon, Mike Tyson told me to take him to DKP so he could pick up the deposit money for the motor coach. I was driving a Range Rover stretch limousine, a demonstrator, that a dealer had loaned us. It was a fifteen-pack, twenty-five feet long, with a white-leather interior, and a 5,000-watt stereo system. The Range Rover people wanted Tyson to try it out and see if he would purchase it for the modest price of $400,000. We showed up at DKP's three-storey brownstone between Park and Madison without advance warning. The only person aware of our impending visit there was the real-estate agent from Brown Harris Stevens.

I parked the pearl-white limo which took up four spaces. Tyson, Anthony Pitts, and I got out and climbed the steps to the front door of Don King Productions. The receptionist buzzed us in. I leaned over the counter and gave her a kiss, and MT said he was taking the elevator to get his check. Tyson was on his way to the second-floor executive offices. The lady from Brown Harris Stevens arrived, and we sat in the lobby reviewing information about The Alfred penthouse my boss was interested in purchasing. About five minutes had passed when the receptionist's intercom crackled loudly, someone yelling that "a fight had broken out" upstairs. I recognized the voice as being that of Celia Tuckman, a DKP executive in charge of its pay-per-view business. She started screaming for the receptionist to call the police.

"Let's go!" I shouted to Anthony, and we bolted up the stairs. I already had visited those offices enough times to be familiar with every detail of their layout. The legal dispute between Bill Cayton and DKP hadn't yet been resolved, and Cayton's contract didn't expire until February 12, 1992. However, for all practical purposes Don King had taken over Mike Tyson's boxing career and personal affairs. King just started dealing directly with MT as if he already had won the battle for control. Of course, John Horne and Rory Holloway, loyal Don King mercenaries, had been assisting him every step of the way.

I really didn't understand what was going on behind the scenes. It wasn't my place to try and get involved. For some time now I had been going to that brownstone on 69th Street. The Don King Productions offices were used to stage interviews and promotional events. I also went there on a regular basis to pick up payroll checks, hundreds of thousands in cash for MT's "expense money," and sealed envelopes containing paperwork for my boss to review. I noticed that these same envelopes would be sealed when I returned them the next day to DKP.

King's office on the second floor of the brownstone had a desk crafted in the shape of a crown. A conference table was attached to it where a dozen people could sit. Behind the desk was a throne done in a gold motif. To the right of the throne was a huge old-style black and gold safe, with a big "wheel" King would spin to open its heavy door, extracting the large sums of cash he often handed out. There also was an array of monitors allowing King to conduct surveillance on every part of the premises both inside and out. Adorning Don King's office were dozens of trophies, awards, and photographs of him posing with famous people, including Presidents Ronald Reagan and George H.W. Bush, foreign political leaders, celebrities, like Michael Jackson and, of course, famous fighters he had promoted over the years like Muhammad Ali. There also were numerous posters, large reproductions of magazine covers, and articles relating to Don King's career.

In addition to King's office on the second floor, there was one for controller Joseph Maffia and one for pay-per-view executive Celia Tuckman. As we rushed into King's office, we immediately noticed that Tyson's opponent two months before, Razor Ruddock, was lying on the floor. His hands were folded on his chest like he was on display inside a coffin at a funeral home. MT had knocked him out cold, unlike the controversial technical knockout he was awarded in the seventh round of the March 18, 1991 fight. Don King was behind his crown-shaped desk, his eyes bugging out in fear, as Mike Tyson started climbing over the conference table to get to him.

We then noticed there were other people in the room. Seated on a sofa were the two ogres known in the boxing business as "the twins" who worked as bodyguards for Ruddock. Murad Muhammad, Ruddock's promoter, also was present. One of the twins jumped up and tried to grab MT because he now had started advancing toward King. The other twin got into a fistfight with Anthony. Failing to reach Tyson, the first twin went for a bag. It looked to me like he was going for a weapon. This wasn't the right time to test my Aikido skills, the Japanese martial art I recently had mastered to help me protect Mike Tyson. Instead, I pulled out my Glock 9mm semi-automatic and shouted "stop!" Then I glanced over at my boss and saw him trying to isolate King behind his desk.

I turned back to the twin whose hand was still in the bag. "Get your fucking hand out of there!"

"I'll kill you!" Tyson shouted at King. "Why's this nigger here? What's he doing in my fucking building?"

Don King was babbling wildly, insisting that Razor Ruddock was there just to discuss the next fight.

"What fight?!" MT kept shouting. "I'm not fighting that nigger! I want Holyfield!"

"Mike, goddammit, you better stop this shit! What the fuck are you talking about? Take it easy!"

"Where's my money? I want all my money now!"

Seeing an opportunity to get away, King sprang from behind his desk, out the door, and into the hallway. Tyson charged out after him.

"I've got these two guys!" Anthony yelled at me. "Get MT! Don't let him do this!"

Don King was hiding out in Celia Tuckman's office. By now most of the DKP staff had made their way to the second floor, trying to figure out what all the commotion was about. Tuckman pleaded with Tyson to stop kicking and punching the walls which had caused a number of pictures to fall to the ground. I came up to MT and told him to forget about King, that the cops were on their way. He didn't pay any attention to me so I grabbed his arm.

"Don't touch me, Rudy! Get the fuck off!"

I started pulling Tyson away from the door. Very angry, but also very embarrassed by what he had done, Mike

Tyson decided to end it. We bolted down the stairs. By the time we reached the lobby, Razor Ruddock, face bloody and still woozy from Tyson's punch, had made it down another staircase. Ruddock went for MT, and they started struggling. He was no match for Tyson who began connecting with punches to Ruddock's mid-section.

I yelled at the receptionist to buzz us out, but she panicked and froze, so I pulled the Glock and shot at the glass. As I opened the door for my boss, he delivered a final roundhouse to Ruddock's head which crumpled the big Jamaican to the floor like a rag doll. Outside, I aimed the keyless remote at the Range Rover limousine. I pushed MT into the limo and locked all the doors to make sure Ruddock would not reach him again. We looked back for Anthony who was still inside. A moment later he appeared at the front door, covered with blood, his face scratched from a brawl with the twins. I lowered the front passenger window and yelled for Anthony to get in. In the distance I noticed Sarah Wallace from WABC's *Eyewitness News*, a cameraman trailing her close behind. They were frantically trying to make their way to the scene.

"Anthony!" I yelled again. "The media's here. Get the fuck in!"

Anthony was still at the front door when one of the twins suddenly appeared and tried to mix it up with him again. He spun around and planted a huge blow on his attacker's face, causing several of the twin's teeth to shoot out onto the sidewalk. Anthony jumped into the front seat, but we still had a slight problem. There were vehicles parked in front and behind us. I didn't have enough space to pull out. Having no choice, I backed up and slammed into the car behind me, pushing it back a few feet. I swung out and hit another vehicle, a black Lincoln limo double-parked next to us, taking off a good chunk of its front end. Sarah Wallace desperately was pursuing us, trying to get our attention, but I peeled rubber, and we were gone in a flash.

One of the twins had bitten Anthony Pitts badly on the hand, and that further upset Tyson. My first priority was to get Anthony some clothes because his were covered with blood. I parked in front of a sporting goods store and ran inside, buying him an extra-large sweat suit and a pair of sneakers in record time. I threw money on the counter and left without waiting for the change. Anthony changed in the back of the limo, and then I found a garbage can where I ditched his blood-soaked clothes.

After he changed, Anthony returned to the front of the limo so our boss could be alone. We talked about what had happened at Don King Productions. Pitts said I had "done good" when I pulled out my Glock and trained it on one of the twins, then convinced MT to leave DKP before he did something very bad he later would regret. Anthony said I had been able "to keep a cool head" while everything was happening so quickly and violently.

Our boss was quiet during the next twenty minutes so I finally lowered the partition to get his instructions. He had dozed off so we just kept driving around. After about an hour our Skypagers went off with messages to contact John Horne and Rory Holloway. Anthony called Horne, and there was a lot of yelling back and forth. Finally, John Horne demanded to know what Mike Tyson was doing right then, and Anthony hung up on him. Our boss woke up a few minutes later, lowered the partition, and stuck his head forward with a wide grin.

"You guys had my back. You guy are my niggers forever. Don't worry what happened there. You work for me." MT reached for Anthony and gave him a hug.

"And, you, you crazy bastard," Mike Tyson said, squeezing my head affectionately, "always looking for an excuse to protect me."

"You're not going to be happy with me, sir, because I smacked up the car."

"Don't worry about it, Rudy," he said. "I don't like it anyway."

We told MT about the pages from John Horne and Rory Holloway, and that they were looking for him.

"I don't wanna talk to those niggers. Don King is gonna pay for this!"

Mike Tyson said he had been upset with Don King talking with Razor Ruddock behind his back. After a few more minutes of discussing what had happened at DKP, MT began joking about the incident. He laughed loudly when he recalled Razor Ruddock "had squealed like a pig." Tyson also thought it was funny he would end up buying the Range Rover, which he really didn't like, because it would cost too much to fix. We headed for the movies at 34th Street on the East Side where MT wanted to see, for the tenth time that year, the original *Ninja Turtles* movie.

Later that afternoon on *WABC*'s five o'clock news, Sarah Wallace aired a piece about the fight at Don King Productions. She displayed a napkin containing the teeth which Anthony Pitts had knocked out that she had been able to recover on the sidewalk. Wallace also showed the blood at the front of the building. A DKP official would deny later that anything out of the ordinary had happened. If that really were the case, then why did Don King go out and purchase a bullet-proof vest that very same day?

***

It wasn't long after the altercation at DKP before John Horne and Rory Holloway showed up to earn their keep by commencing the healing process between Mike Tyson and Don King. They were smart enough to wait a couple of days while MT continued to cool down. Then they appeared at the Marlborough House and tried to convince Tyson there was absolutely nothing wrong with what he had seen and heard a few days before at DKP. Horne and Holloway spent a lot of time talking about how dumb it would be to fight Evander Holyfield now because "the world was convinced that Razor Ruddock was badder than Holyfield." As it usually turned out, their non-stop blabber got results, and Mike Tyson was back on track for the next Razor Ruddock fight.

Word got back to MT that Pope John Paul wanted to meet him. Once Tyson had traveled to Rome with Naomi Campbell, but the Pope found out too late about his presence in the Eternal City. A big Mike Tyson fan, the Pope later extended an open invitation to him for a papal visit. Because my boss was ripe at this moment for getting away from it all, he told me to contact the Vatican and make arrangements for us to fly to Rome.

Don King felt very insecure after he learned Mike Tyson would be spending time in Europe far away from John Horne and Rory Holloway. So he decided to round up the troops, Horne, Holloway, their wives, and DKP executive Celia Tuckman, and they headed to Rome. After Don King located us, he organized a trip to Poland for the entire group. Apparently, he had been very interested for awhile in visiting a certain location in that country. At the time we didn't have anything else to do so MT agreed to make the journey. King chartered a private jet, and we all climbed aboard, destination Auschwitz, the most notorious of all Nazi death camps. I had heard that Don King already had visited Dachau and other concentration camps on previous trips to Europe.

As he walked around Auschwitz, Don King appeared very animated. It had become pretty clear to me over time that he had studied the history of the Nazi movement and was interested in its propaganda techniques. I also learned he possessed a collection of Nazi memorabilia. At his townhouse in midtown Manhattan, I had seen display cases filled with swastikas and other Nazi items. Before we left Auschwitz, Don King gathered up some of the earth and rocks to take them back to the United States.

During the more than four years that I had known him, I had only seen Mike Tyson cry twice. One time was at the funeral of his sister, Denise. The other was at the funeral of his co-manager, close friend, and confidante, Jim Jacobs. Now, as he toured the most gruesome death camp in the history of mankind, and for the first time really understood what the Nazi "final solution" was all about, Mike Tyson could not hold back the tears.

***

In preparation for the Tyson-Ruddock rematch on June 28, 1991, we reestablished our training camp in Las Vegas. However, much to our surprise, this time we would not be living in a luxurious penthouse at The Mirage. Steve Wynn had been extremely attentive to our needs. Every issue which had arisen had been quickly, effectively, and courteously resolved by Mr. Wynn and his top-notch staff. At all times they genuinely seemed to be proud to have us around The Mirage. We had conducted ourselves properly and were not aware of any problems. But Don King told us that Steve Wynn didn't want us to stay at The Mirage anymore. According to King, Mr. Wynn claimed that we had given the hotel a bad reputation "running around there." I soon would discover what King had said was a vicious lie designed to distance my boss from Steve Wynn, a gracious host and loyal Mike Tyson fan.

"The Mirage don't want no niggers running around there," Don King claimed. "So you niggers are going to use the house Mike bought in Vegas. You don't need to be hanging around those white people who don't want no niggers hanging around their places. And you," he added, staring at me, "you're just a nigger with straight hair."

Don King had arranged for Mike Tyson to purchase a house in the Las Vegas Country Club Estates. It had six bedrooms, six bathrooms, a swimming pool, gym, and gourmet kitchen. The property was located next to a golf course behind the Hilton Hotel and was surrounded by a wall. I had a room at a nearby motel which I could use to crash during sporadic, brief periods when I wasn't required to be with MT. Richie Giachetti, who took over Tyson's training after Kevin Rooney was fired, also had a room at that motel. Giachetti was a good and simple man, one of the best trainers in the business.

Mike Tyson accepted what Don King had told him about Steve Wynn and The Mirage, just as he had done so many times before. Using his mercenaries, John Horne and

Rory Holloway, King had an uncanny ability to erase almost any distrust or disgust for "Daddy King" which Tyson felt from time to time. I remember the many hours we had spent, at Don King's insistence, watching World War II documentaries, and how mass propaganda seemed to hypnotize the German people, making them zombie-like as they listened to their Fuhrer, Adolf Hitler. If someone tells you something enough times, you will start to believe it. It didn't take a genius to figure out that's how Don King continued to hold Mike Tyson in his grip for so long. King's program was made even easier because Tyson had a handicap about which I was not aware until a short time later. It was only then that I fully could understand why Mike Tyson was so easily convinced by John Horne and Rory Holloway to do things against his best interests, and why his periodic rages against Don King seemed to subside almost as quickly as they had arisen.

While Mike Tyson was living in a house, King, Horne, Holloway, and the DKP staff took up residence at The Mirage. King occupied the same luxurious penthouse suite Steve Wynn had provided my boss while he prepared for the first Ruddock fight. Horne and Holloway were given an adjoining suite. King took over space in the hotel to run DKP's operations and brought in some of his staff, including Joseph Maffia, Celia Tuckman, and Gladys Rosa. It became obvious that King was trying to keep MT away from The Mirage and Steve Wynn as much as possible.

I would continue to stop by The Mirage whenever I got a chance because I still had several girlfriends who worked there. That's how I learned that King's explanation to us had been a huge deception designed to distance Mike

Tyson from Steve Wynn. My girlfriends also had been very surprised that we hadn't set up shop in the hotel just like before. They told me that Mr. Wynn, and everybody else at The Mirage, had been delighted to have us reside on the premises. Our presence had brought additional prestige and excitement to the resort's already super-charged atmosphere. Mike Tyson was happy to shake hands with hotel guests and handed out autographs wherever he might be. None of my girlfriends could recall a bad word being said about MT, Anthony Pitts, or me.

The truth was that Don King believed Mike Tyson was getting too chummy with Steve Wynn. The Mirage already had shown an interest in promoting fights on its own even before King came into the picture. And with Mike Tyson spending an extended period of time at The Mirage, his luxury automobiles parked in front as if it were his own driveway, Don King was very worried "his fighter" might develop a direct and close relationship with a very powerful competitor. To prevent this unacceptable possibility from happening, King and his intimates established themselves at The Mirage while Tyson was stashed away at a safe distance from the hotel and Steve Wynn.

Everything appeared to be going smoothly with less than a month remaining before Tyson-Ruddock II. I was supervising the organization and maintenance of the house in the Country Club Estates. MT was training well under the very capable eye of Richie Giachetti, and there was a lot of quiet time. Giachetti implemented a training schedule, which included a 7 p.m. curfew, so Tyson would be rested and ready to arise at 5 a.m. for his daily five-mile jog before the desert sun came up. Giachetti mapped out a route with hills to increase Tyson's endurance.

There did come a point in time when the spartan schedule Giachetti had imposed finally became unbearable for my boss who longed to visit some of his girlfriends in Los Angeles. As much as possible, my job was to be with MT around the clock. When he was training, this meant also being Tyson's babysitter to make sure he didn't violate the training rules and nightly curfews. Because Las Vegas had such an exciting nightlife, nobody else was willing to help me out. Therefore, by the early evening, I usually was ready to hit the sack.

One night MT woke me up around 8 p.m. and told me he was going to sneak out and go to Los Angeles, a 300-mile, four-hour drive, to see a girlfriend. I figured he was going to do it whether he had my blessing or not, and it would be safer if I went along. I pulled out the $750,000 Ferrari F40 Koenig which had a twelve-cylinder 750 hp twin turbo-charged engine. This vehicle was nothing short of a rocket on wheels. Keeping in mind that we would have to make the round-trip in incredibly short time, we headed west at speeds up to 190 m.p.h. MT had paid a lot of money for me to attend a school in Phoenix where I was able to qualify as a Formula One race-car driver. I also studied defensive driving techniques. Mike Tyson loved speeding along the highway, and he sure got his money's worth that night. With the oversize super-wide rear tires, I was taking turns at 100 m.p.h. We made LA in under 2-1/2 hours, MT hooked up with his lady friend, and we were back at the Vegas house around 3 a.m. Incredibly, during our round-trip we never encountered the highway patrol. Of course, if there had been any units lying-in-wait, they would have realized there was no way they were going to catch up to us.

My boss had such a good time on that first trip where he snuck out that he decided to risk it a few more times. The plan was that around 8:00 p.m. I would leave a note at the front gate stating nobody was to enter the premises. After that I would pull out the Ferrari, and MT would jump in, ducking down so that Richie Giachetti, or anybody else spying on the house, would think that I was alone. If things went according to schedule, we would arrive in Los Angeles by 11 p.m., party for an hour or so, then be back in Vegas by 3 a.m. Giachetti would awaken Tyson at 5 a.m. to do his five-mile jog. The human body, even that of Mike Tyson, has certain limits, and it soon became apparent something was wrong. MT was showing signs of weakness in the gym, and he was hobbling and wobbling more than jogging. He made up the story that he had been suffering from insomnia. Giachetti didn't buy it, and one day he pulled me aside.

"Don't bullshit me, Rudy!" he snapped. "I had a look at the mufflers on that Ferrari."

I knew what Tyson's lead trainer was talking about. Those mufflers must have looked like burnt marshmallows. At 190 m.p.h. hurtling across the desert highway, the Ferrari Koenig spit fire. You could see the road behind us glowing red. Richie Giachetti was very concerned about our fighter being in top shape when he went up against Razor Ruddock in the rematch which was only a few weeks away. Since the days of Cus D'Amato, Mike Tyson had been taught that one of the keys to being a top athlete was getting enough rest. Any partying that had been going on had to stop immediately, and my boss was going to be in bed by 8 p.m. every evening. If those instructions were not followed,

Giachetti was going to make me pay a fine for each violation. I reported back to MT that our elaborate charade had been discovered, and that Richie Giachetti was going to kick our asses if it ever happened again. Tyson agreed that he "better chill out" and called off the LA trip he had been planning for that evening.

I decided to take a night off since we weren't going to be up to any mischief. However, Anthony's fiancée had come into town, as she would do on many weekends, so I agreed to give them some time alone. Although my boss said he was going to crash, there was something in his voice that made me suspicious. After awhile, lying on the living room sofa half-asleep in pitch darkness, I thought ghosts were flying by me. When I finally focused my eyes, I realized it was a butt-naked Tyson with a black chick hurrying toward the staircase. A few minutes later there was some very loud moaning upstairs. I climbed the steps, opened the door to his bedroom, and poked my head inside. Although it was dark, I could make out the shapes of two bodies lying on the floor on the black sable "bedspread" which my boss had purchased in Moscow.

"Hey, what's up?"

"Hey, man, just trying to get some sleep." Tyson thought I still didn't know about the girl.

"Sir, please do me a favor. When you've finished doing the wild thing with that black ghost next to you, please send her home so Giachetti doesn't dock my pay."

Tyson thought this comment was so funny that he rolled over and burst out into uncontrollable laughter. The next morning I went out and bought alarms for each door of the house. That night I found myself babysitting Tyson again because everybody else already had plans. The door alarms were installed so at least I wasn't expecting a repeat of the previous night.

"You're not going to have any more ghosts walking around again, are you?" I asked out of caution anyway.

"Why don't you just take all those damn door alarms, Rudy," Tyson said, "and shove them up your ass." Tyson laughed and went upstairs.

Finally, I was getting some sleep when I heard a big smack on the ground outside. I hit the emergency switch which triggered the lights all around the property. I rushed out the front door and noticed MT tangled up in a thorny bush. In an attempt to sneak out of the house without me knowing, he had fallen from the second floor. If he hadn't been caught, he was going to roll the Ferrari silently down the driveway and into the street to complete his getaway. I started helping MT pluck the thorns out of his butt.

"Damn, I'm okay," he said in disgust waving me away. "Shit, man, I was gonna get laid."

I realized my boss was going to keep pulling this crap. If he escaped, and I wasn't with him, he'd most likely get into worse trouble. And that was going to cost me, not just some money, but probably my job.

"Sir, if you're going to do this shit, at least take me with you. I work for you, not your career."

I made a big mistake by saying that. The next night we were back on the road to Los Angeles. Finally, about two weeks before Tyson-Ruddock II, my boss realized that it was time to stop this craziness and concentrate only on the upcoming fight.

The Ferrari Koenig wasn't designed for people like us

but rather to be taken to the racetrack once a month. However, Tyson loved that car so much he didn't care. We used to wear racing helmets because the Koenig didn't have a roof and, if bugs hit us at such high speeds, they could knock us out like a Tyson punch to the temple. Rick Black, owner of Black On Black Imports in Beverly Hills, did his best to assist us with servicing and repairing this vehicle. The Koenig had to be stripped down completely fairly often, just like a professional racing car after a major competition, which always cost a bundle. One day MT hit a speed bump too hard causing damage to its front end. It took three weeks to repair the Koenig, and it set Tyson back $180,000. Another time he was showing off the car to a girlfriend, popped the clutch, and snapped the drive shaft. Rick Black was at the end of his rope with us. He ordered a special titanium drive shaft which we wouldn't be able to break except by nuclear fission.

MT finally got fed up with the Koenig, realizing it wasn't practical to use and was costing too much to maintain and repair. But that car had been his pride and joy so I came up with a wild idea and had the car shipped to his Ohio estate. After King took over Tyson's life, he convinced "his fighter" to buy a residence near his own just east of Cleveland. King owned 2,000 acres there and had a thirty-room mansion complete with greenhouse and tennis courts. He adorned the mansion with an American flag, another with the word "Liberty," and a third with the DKP crown logo and the phrase "Only in America." King just happened to have the right property for MT in nearby Southington, 29,000 square feet under roof with a massive game room. Anthony thought I had gone nuts when he learned about my scheme. Without first securing MT's permission, I hired a contractor to knock a big hole in one of the game room's exterior walls.

"You're on your own!" said Anthony, not wanting any part of this "surprise," certain that I would be fired.

When MT returned to the Southington Estate, he discovered the Ferrari F40 Koenig mounted like a model airplane on a platform in the middle of the huge game room. He literally freaked out, having assumed this car he loved so much had been sent to storage never to be seen again.

"This is the baddest thing around!" Tyson shouted out. And then I knew that I still had my job.

"Just Sign Here"

"Just Sign Here"

On June 12, 1991, the temperature in Las Vegas was hovering around 115 degrees as we returned from the afternoon training session with Richie Giachetti. With just sixteen days left before Tyson-Ruddock II, MT was really buckling down for this important rematch. That afternoon he had knocked out three sparring partners. My boss had committed himself to end the controversy about the first Razor Ruddock fight by decisively crushing his opponent this time around. He then would take on Evander "Real Deal" Holyfield and regain the heavyweight championship crown. No longer would anybody delay Mike Tyson's true destiny, Don King and company included.

With it being so hot, I had planned to jump into the pool with my clothes on. MT said he was going upstairs to take a shower, rest, and watch some cartoons. When he saw us enter the house, the new chef, Hans Strauss, started whipping up the protein shakes which Tyson would chug down by the pitcherful. A four-star chef who had worked for a number of celebrities, Strauss had replaced Chef Early. Don King fired Chef Early allegedly for "sneaking out the back door with meat" from Mike Tyson's residence. I never believed that bullshit excuse because Chef Early was a very honorable man. MT used to have a lot of fun with the tall, distinguished master cook of soul food, spending many hours shooting craps with him on the kitchen floor. They had a deal that, if Tyson won, he would get some greasy food, like fried chicken or pork ribs, even if he was on a training diet. Chef Early's presence was sorely missed by all of us, especially my boss.

Much later, sometime in 1993, I learned the real reason why Don King had dismissed MT's favorite chef and crap-shooting buddy. I was in a subway station in New York wearing one of my elegant "Team Tyson" leather jackets. A young black man approached me and said he was a nephew of Chef Early. He gave me the telephone number for his uncle at Chef Early Caterers on East Flatbush in Brooklyn. I called the next day and spoke with our old friend.

"I got fired because I wouldn't put that magic powder in Mike's food," Chef Early said.

I had no idea what the hell he was talking about. Chef Early told me the shocking story. John Horne had given him a powder to be added to Tyson's food. The powder supposedly was an "endurance vitamin." Horne instructed the chef to keep this to himself because, although it was "absolutely necessary" for his training regimen, MT had been refusing to take this substance. Chef Early didn't like this explanation and didn't want to put anything extra into MT's food without him or me knowing about it. Moreover, when the chef had a closer look at this "vitamin powder," he found a tiny piece of an orange capsule stamped with an "S" or "5." After Chef Early refused to follow John Horne's order, Don King gave Tyson's favorite cook his walking papers.

I spoke with a pharmacist and mentioned that at one time Tyson had been taking Thorazine and Lithium. He told me what Chef Early had discovered in the "vitamin powder" could have been part of a Thorazine capsule. That drug was one of the anti-depressants administered to Mike Tyson after Ruth Roper and Robin Givens had packed him off to a psychiatrist. That same psychiatrist later agreed that Tyson wasn't suffering from any mental disorder. Thorazine was one of the medications Tyson had been taking the night of the infamous *20/20* interview where he had looked so sheepish and foolish in front of the camera. I later checked with a psychiatrist who told me the drug worked like a sedative if administered to a person who didn't have a psychiatric problem. Chef Early didn't get in touch with Mike Tyson after Don King fired him. However, it wasn't easy to reach out to us because our phone numbers constantly were changing after King took over every aspect of Tyson's career. In one three-month period, Don King Productions changed our telephone numbers six times supposedly for "our own protection."

Our new chef, Hans Strauss, mentioned to me that earlier in the afternoon John Horne had left a large, sealed envelope on the long, black-marble dining room table. As usual, I would give MT these envelopes, which contained paperwork for his review, and then return them to Don King Productions. Strauss said the envelope was to be sent back right away to the DKP offices at The Mirage. When I took the envelope upstairs, I noticed my boss was on the phone. He was doodling on a notepad, CDs and clothes strewn all over the floor. Tyson had been playing with one of his most important possessions, a miniature train set purchased after the first Razor Ruddock fight. The set cost $5,000 and fit into a steamer trunk which had built-in tracks, mountains, and tunnels. I dropped the big envelope on the bed and left. I changed my clothes and jumped into the pool where I remained for about thirty minutes. After I got out and dried off, I asked Chef Strauss to make me my favorite meal, barbecued seafood. Just then one of our Mexican maids marched toward me.

"I'm not going to do this job anymore, señor Rudy!" she said in Spanish, obviously very upset. "He's an animal! He's throwing papers all over the room. I'm tired of always straightening up after him!"

Two of our employees, another maid and the gardener, heard this commotion and came to the kitchen.

"Don't leave yet," I said, trying to calm her down. "Let me see what's going on first."

I wasn't happy that my seafood barbecue plans were being interrupted by another Tyson temper tantrum. I was surprised that MT was having one that afternoon because things had been pretty peaceful now that his training was in high gear for the Tyson-Ruddock rematch. I bolted up the stairs, then slowly opened the bedroom door. Now there wasn't just a mess of CDs and clothes all over the place but also a lot of papers and checks and pieces of broken items. While talking on the phone, MT continued flinging things around the room. Thinking about the big hassle of having to replace a good maid just because Tyson suddenly had developed an attitude, I lost control.

"What's going on!" I yelled at him, the first time I ever had done that since going to work for him. "I'm tired of you doing this shit! One of our maids just quit. Why are there papers all over the place?"

Mike Tyson's eyes were bugging out wildly as he suddenly lunged at me, grabbing my shirt and pulling me toward him. I hadn't expected this because my boss never had done anything like that in five years. I was trained in the Japanese martial art of Aikido, but I still was scared shitless. Tyson could break me in half in two seconds if he wanted. I relaxed, showing him I wasn't going to resist.

"Rudy, I can't read, man," he said, his eyes watery. "Don is fucking macking me! All I do is keep signing. I'm tired of signing."

Since I first met him in November of 1986, I never knew this about Mike Tyson. Then it hit me like a ton of bricks. At a fancy restaurant, Tyson would review the menu but end up saying "just order me whatever's best." He would look at newspapers but only the comic strips. MT signed his name when he handed out autographs, but the only other type of writing I had seen from him was "doodling."

"Don't worry about it," I told him. "I'll read with you. I'll help you. Just calm down. We're gonna work it out together." I reassured my boss that we would find a way to understand all these checks and documents. "I'll pick this stuff up. Breaking shit ain't gonna help."

Mike Tyson released me, and I began gathering up all the stuff from the package Horne had delivered earlier in the day. A lot of checks were stapled to Don King Productions memos. Everything appeared to be official business. But as I started taking a closer look, I noticed many checks had dollar amounts written in but otherwise were left blank. One of the checks which did have a payee was made out to "Centel," a cellular phone company, in an amount over $100,000. I got very scared because that was my mobile phone company, the only person on Team Tyson who had a "flip-phone" from Centel. MT was going to think I had gone berserk, talking to my girlfriends for way too many hours. But even if I had done that, it would have impossible to spend more than $100,000 in one month! No invoices were attached to this check, only a memo instructing Tyson to "just sign and return." I had no idea what accounts related to this Centel payment. MT asked me what I was doing while I was rummaging through all these papers.

"We've got to contact Joe Maffia," I said. "We've got to demand invoices to know what you're paying. Like this Centel thing."

"That's our phones, right?"

"No way, Sir! We only have one phone from that company. I don't want you to blame me for this huge bill. You don't have a $100,000 phone bill!"

MT was boiling. "Don King is stealing from me!"

It was around 5 p.m. in New York, still time enough to catch the comptroller at DKP. There never had been any problems between Maffia and me during our frequent dealings. Except for that one time relating to the deposit for the Genesis motorcoach, Joseph Maffia always had been pleasant whenever I needed to make arrangements to pay for MT's purchases. When he picked up the phone, the DKP comptroller seemed happy to hear from me.

"MT wants invoices," I told Maffia, "for each item in the June package."

For a few moments there was dead silence at the other end. "Rudy," he finally said, "what are you doing?"

"MT said there's checks for huge amounts of money and no invoices."

Again there was a dead silence, but this time it was longer. "My God, Rudy, what have you done?" Joseph Maffia finally said in a very cold, low voice.

"Joe, I'm here with MT, and he wants me to take over the billing process starting now."

"I can't do nothing until I talk to Don," Maffia said, and then the line went dead.

Tyson got very agitated when Maffia hung up on us because he hadn't been able to get information on his own monthly expenses unless Don King gave his approval.

"Rudy, call that nigger back," MT instructed me, "and put me on the phone."

When I called Don King Productions again, I was put on hold for several minutes.

"MT wants to talk to you," I told Joe Maffia when he finally picked up, then handed the phone to my boss.

"If you don't want me to get on a plane and break your fucking face," Tyson barked, "fax what Rudy wants now, starting with the Centel bill!" Then my boss slammed the phone down hard.

Mike Tyson looked over at me with an expression of relief, like a great weight had been taken off his shoulders. He was awakening from a deep, coma-like sleep. My boss finally had someone who was going to help him get answers to all the checks which had been shoved in his face for him to sign ever since Don King took over his affairs. And maybe he also looked relieved because he finally had confessed, to someone he trusted within his inner ring, that he couldn't read. I always had assumed that MT read and understood the contents of all those sealed envelopes which were delivered to him and then returned by hand to Don King Productions. This was mostly done by John Horne. After all, my boss was the president of his own corporation, Mike Tyson Productions. But now I realized that MT had been living with a painful, silent handicap for a very long time. And it was this handicap, which he had been too embarrassed to admit, that had given others a blank check to mislead and deceive and commit fraud upon Mike Tyson.

***

It only took a few minutes before the fax beeped, announcing documents were on their way from New York. By then I had looked at a lot more checks. I was stunned to find that Mike Tyson was being billed for living and training in his own camp. There was a check made out from Mike Tyson Productions to Don King Productions for $300,000, the notation on the line in the lower-left-hand corner "living expenses." How could Mike Tyson be paying $300,000 a month to live on property he supposedly owned outright? It got much worse as we reviewed other checks Mike Tyson Productions had issued. There was one to Don King's daughter for $2,000, salary for her serving as vice-president of "The Mike Tyson Fan Club." Another was to Henrietta King for consulting fees of $100,000 even though she never did anything for Mike Tyson. In fact, King family members rarely even took the time to say hello to my boss when they happened to be around. And then there were the John Horne and Rory Holloway checks in the amount of $400,000 each. The memo portion of these checks contained a simple line through them as if to say "nothing in particular."

I began to carefully review the Centel invoice as the fax machine continued spitting it out. Mike Tyson was being billed for the cellular phones and Skypagers of the entire staff of Don King Productions, members of Don King's family, and other individuals who had no affiliation with Mike Tyson Productions. The names included John Horne, Rory

Holloway, Joseph Maffia, King's son Carl, secretary Coylette James, executive assistant Dana Jamison, Latin boxing executive Gladys Rosa, bodyguard Jerome Jordan, media director Joe Safety, Holloway's brother Todd, in-house courier Coy Sparks, and King's chauffeur Captain Joe. There should have been only three names on that invoice, Mike Tyson, Anthony Pitts, and Rudy Gonzalez, because we were the only persons who worked for Mike Tyson Productions.

Sitting there surrounded by this mountain of checks and papers, we realized that Mike Tyson Productions, in the month of June alone, was about to shell out nearly $1.5 million in expenses which shouldn't have been billed to it at all. A professional boxer pays his manager a percentage of his fight revenue and, in exchange, the manager has to perform certain services at his own expense. The fight promoter gets a percentage of fight revenue, an amount controlled by boxing regulators. If the promoter has a staff, he pays them out of his own revenue. Otherwise, the boxer would end up paying twice. I remembered the times when my boss would meet with his former co-managers, Jim Jacobs and Bill Cayton. They would explain in detail what was being spent and why. With Jacobs and Cayton, there had been receipts and formalities. With Don King, Mike Tyson simply had become a blank check.

***

We sat on the bedroom floor going over the checks and documents for what seemed like hours. In fact, only a few minutes had passed. We discovered more expenses which never should have been billed to Mike Tyson Productions. Don King Productions had prepared checks for MT to sign relating to the rental of three New York apartments. They were for Celia Tuckman and two other DKP employees. One had a monthly price tag of $12,000, another $8,000. While we were reviewing these expenses, we heard a big commotion downstairs. A few moments later, Don King and John Horne stormed into the bedroom. Obviously, someone had made those two aware of our transcontinental demand for documentation.

Mike Tyson jumped up and shook a finger at Don King. "I'm through with you, motherfucker! You've been stealing my money!"

King glared in my direction. "Don't listen to this fucking kid!"

"No, he's not lying. He just sat down and been reading with me all this shit I been signing. Why am I paying your family?"

Tyson started grabbing anything in sight and went on a smashing rampage, then wheeled around and knocked John Horne to the ground.

"You've known about this shit!" he screamed at Horne who lay in a silent heap, waiting for "Daddy King" to resolve the crisis as he always had done before.

"Go downstairs, motherfucker," said King, cocking his head toward me.

As I turned to leave, Mike Tyson disappeared inside the bathroom and slammed the door. I headed downstairs and noticed the curious staff gathered below. Outside I sat on the black Lamborghini Diablo parked in the driveway. Suddenly, I got very scared about what I had started less than an hour before. There had been rumblings for some time about Don King's ripoffs of other fighters such as Muhammad Ali and Larry Holmes. In fact, we had been experiencing our own whispers from the darkness of the Kingdom, like that day we had arrived unannounced at DKP to pick up the Genesis deposit check. It was more than three weeks later, and we still didn't have the money. After a few minutes, John Horne walked out of the house and quietly ordered me to go to my room at the Sheffield Inn and await further instructions.

"I don't want to look at you anymore," he added.

I opened the door to the Diablo and started to climb inside.

"Give me the keys," Horne said. "You can't use the Lamborghini. Mike doesn't want anybody using his cars."

"Fuck you, John Horne!" I fired up the Diablo and laid rubber, kicking up dirt and gravel behind me, some of which smacked Horne right in the face.

If I had stayed a moment longer, I probably would have started severely kicking that lowly weasel's ass. After I arrived at the Sheffield Inn a few minutes later, I received a call from Anthony Pitts.

"Yo, what did you do, man? You brought down the house. MT wants to talk to you."

"What are you doing in your motel room?" Mike Tyson asked me.

"I'm sorry, sir. John Horne told me to come over here. I'm sorry for everything."

"Don't apologize, Rudy," MT said. "Take the rest of the afternoon off. I'm throwing Anthony out too. I wanna think this over. Call me tomorrow. I wanna be alone now."

That night I drove the Diablo to The Mirage where I picked up one of my girlfriends, Candy, a blackjack dealer from Bogota, Colombia. We drove to Boulder City which was about twenty-five miles southeast of Las Vegas. When we got back to my place, Candy spent the night with me. The next morning I returned to Tyson's house to assess the damage. It was a real wreck, in much worse shape than I had left it. I had a long day ahead of me.

We didn't hear a peep from Don King, John Horne, or Rory Holloway for several days. Things went back to "normal" as MT continued to train rigorously with Richie Giachetti. I could tell that my boss felt much closer to me after what had transpired in the house on June 12, 1991.

"I'm either gonna fight Holyfield or retire, Rudy," Tyson said. "I'm tired of the abuse."

A few days before, I had visited The Sharper Image in downtown Las Vegas. There I purchased a Panasonic pocket-size device you could hold in your hand and "scan" any document you wanted to copy.

On the evening of June 18, 1991, Anthony took the "graveyard shift," 9 p.m. to 6 a.m. I had the Lamborghini Diablo because I had been detailing it and getting it back into mint condition. With Anthony babysitting Tyson that night, I decided to sleep in my room at the Sheffield Inn. At The Mirage I picked up Vanessa, another one of my girlfriends employed there. She had emigrated from Cuba and had a job working one of the crap tables. We ended up partying all night. It was around 8 a.m. the next morning, while I was in a deep sleep, when my cellular phone rang. It was Dana Jamison, Don King's executive assistant.

"Rudy, Don wants you to go pick up his new Bentley coupe in LA and bring it here. Captain Joe is sick. He's taking medication so he can't drive. Don knows you're a good driver and won't smash up his new car."

As far as I was concerned, I only had one master, and his name was Mike Tyson. I informed Jamison that, if MT wanted me to run this errand, then fine. She suggested that I stop reporting to Mike Tyson.

"Rudy, you still don't get it, do you? Everybody works for Don King. Even Mike. So why don't you just do what we tell you to do and stop creating problems?"

I wasn't going anywhere without MT's permission and went back to sleep. About an hour later, the motel phone rang. It was John Horne.

"Why aren't you up yet? You're supposed to be ready to go to LA. And I also want you to pick up two jackets for Whitney Houston and her mom and take them to Jeff Hamilton."

John Horne explained the famous singer was in town for a performance. She also was going to attend the Tyson-Ruddock rematch. Whitney Houston's mother had a home in Las Vegas. There had been problems with their Jeff Hamilton leather jackets. Houston's jacket was the wrong size, and her mother's jacket had an error in the spelling of her name. I told Horne the same thing I had said to Dana Jamison.

"Rudy, I'm here with MT right now. Now get the fuck on a plane and go to fucking LA right now and do what you're told to do!"

I got Vanessa out of bed, and we dressed quickly and left the Sheffield Inn. Because I wasn't about to leave a $450,000 Tyson exotic car in the airport parking lot, I had to return to MT's house. I paged Anthony who responded by walkie talkie, a communications system we also used which had about a ten-mile range.

"I need you to take me to the airport. I can't leave the Diablo there. Meet me at the house right away."

By the time I arrived, Anthony's yellow Corvette already was parked in the driveway. We had rented three Corvettes in Vegas, and I also had the use of one of them. I opened the front door, expecting to find my boss. Instead, John Horne was sitting in the living room, a look of shock coming over his face.

"What are you doing here? You're supposed to be in LA!"

"Where's MT?"

"Upstairs sleeping. Don't bother him. Go get Don King's car now. He needs it right away!"

Anthony took me to pick up the Jeff Hamilton jackets and then got me to McCarran International Airport in time to grab an 11:00 a.m. flight to Los Angeles. Anthony and I had become good friends, having spent so much time together over the past few years. We were prepared to give our lives for each other, and we were bound by a simple code of honor: "safe passage for Mike Tyson."

I did two things that morning before I left Vegas for Los Angeles. First, my routine practice would have been to take the keys to the Lamborghini Diablo with me. But that day, when nobody was looking, I stuck them in one the kitchen cookie jars. Second, I placed a call to Daisy, one of my former girlfriends, an ex-stripper who lived in Los Angeles. I told her to pick me up at the airport so I wouldn't have to hassle with arrangements to get around town. She agreed to do that in exchange for a promise of wild sex. Those two things, I soon would find out, would save my life later that day.

"Final Errands"

"Final Errands"

After the forty-minute flight to Los Angeles, I was met by my lady friend, Daisy, who was waiting for me at the gate. The former stripper was in her late forties but was looking great. We had met a few months before on a connecting flight to Los Angeles. At that time I didn't know Daisy was related in some way to Gladys Rosa, a Don King Productions executive. We jumped into Daisy's Mustang and headed for a nearby Holiday Inn where we ended up staying for three hours. After that we headed to Tyson's Wilshire Boulevard apartment where I needed to retrieve a diamond Rolex watch and two bags of Gianni Versace clothing. I instructed Daisy to park the Mustang in the garage and wait for me in the lobby. It was a beautiful sunny day so we decided to walk to the Beverly Hills Rolls-Royce dealership.

Dressed in a two-piece Versace silk pajama-suit, I looked the part of someone who just had purchased a very expensive luxury automobile. Don King had ordered a canary-yellow Bentley Continental R with white interior, yellow piping, and a gold steering wheel bearing the Don King Productions gold-crown logo in its center. This ultra-exclusive, luxury coupé also had gold-crown logos on the door. The paint job was so beautiful you wanted to lick it. The car's hood ornament was encrusted with diamonds Obviously, this was not the kind of vehicle you could ever leave on the street unattended. There had been talk that Don

King was going to design special-edition luxury automobiles and sell the idea to Rolls-Royce.

After the paperwork was completed, I drove the Bentley across the street to the Lamborghini dealership. They had the custom luggage which came with Tyson's Diablo but which hadn't been ready when we took original delivery. After picking up these items, we continued on our way to Jeff Hamilton's factory.

Back in 1987 I had learned that Jeff Hamilton made leather jackets for many celebrities with prices ranging from $5,000 to $100,000. A few years before, Jeff had become famous as the founder of "Guess Jeans for Men." In 1989, I met him for the first time when my boss had me fitted for five jackets with matching pants. Tyson didn't want me wearing a regular chauffeur uniform. Instead, he wanted to have the baddest-looking chauffeur around. Over the years I continued to maintain my friendship with Jeff. Although well-known and wealthy, Jeff Hamilton always was extremely considerate and sincere, a refreshing contrast to most of the celebrities I had met.

Daisy and I were trading dirty jokes as the traffic inched along when my Skypager went off. It logged in the number for Don King Productions in Las Vegas. At the end of the number was the message "911-911," meaning "call immediately!" I made several unsuccessful attempts to reach DKP on my cellular. Although the Bentley had a built-in phone, it hadn't yet been activated. Seconds later I got another page exactly like the first. Now I was getting very concerned about reaching the office right away. In light of what had been happening during the past few days, I was particularly worried. And there I was in the middle of a classic LA traffic jam without immediate phone access.

I turned right onto Beverly Hills Drive, heading in the direction of West Pico Boulevard. I spotted a carwash at the corner, pulled up to a bank of three payphones, and parked. I climbed out and walked about five feet to the phones. Using my long-distance calling card, I dialed the number for DKP at The Mirage. Dana Jamison answered.

"Why is John Horne fucking beeping me 911-911? I already picked up Don King's Bentley."

"I didn't page you, Rudy," she said defensively. "And I'm the only one in the office. Everybody's out at MT's house."

I was pissed about being delayed on my way to see Jeff Hamilton. "If anybody calls, tell them I'm on my way back to Vegas. I already picked up a few things for MT."

"No problem," said Jamison.

I hung up and dialed Jeff Hamilton. He was out of the office attending an NBA playoff game. However, he had alerted his staff to be ready to accommodate me and repair the Whitney Houston jackets.

"We'll fix things up for you no matter how long it takes," his secretary told me.

I hung up and started walking back to the Bentley. On my right side, I noticed the presence of a short young black male about five yards away.

"Yo, mister, that's a bad car you got there!"

"Thanks," I said as I kept walking, the keys to the Bentley in my hand. I was a step away from getting back into the car when he shouted out again.

"Yo, man!"

I turned sideways to see what was the deal. The guy

had advanced to within six feet and was aiming a handgun at my head. There were a few beats of silence. He hadn't asked for my wallet or jewelry or even the keys to the $300,000 luxury automobile. I knew then that he was just going to shoot me for no reason. Out of fear or training, or both, I did whatever I could to protect my head, ducking and covering it with my arm. At that instant the assailant started firing. The first bullet entered my elbow, the second one tore through the bicep. Both shots drove me back against the driver's side door. One of my arteries had been destroyed by these two shots, and blood was spurting from it like a high-pressure hose. Having lost all control of my arm, it now hung limply at my side.

Inside the Bentley, Daisy became hysterical as my blood spattered against the window like wind-driven red rain. Incredibly, I wasn't feeling any pain yet. Instead, I had the sensation everything around me was happening in slow motion. As I slammed against the door I spun around and heard another shot. This bullet struck me in the upper groin, ricocheted off my dragon-shaped belt buckle, then lodged itself in the thick Versace leather. If it weren't for the belt buckle, the third bullet would have ripped open my stomach. I began to lose consciousness and slid slowly down the side of the door until I was sitting on the ground. In the distance I could see my attacker running away.

My brain screamed: "Don't stay there!" I struggled to a crouching position and opened the door. Daisy still was hysterical. Now, inside the Bentley, I was dousing her with blood from my torn artery. Somehow I managed to start the car and take off. The next thing I remembered was a man in a station wagon yelling at us, indicating where there was a hospital nearby. Realizing that I was fading fast, Daisy got me to stop the car. She jumped out and ran around to the driver's side. She pushed me over and got behind the wheel. By now Daisy's face was completely covered with blood as she sped toward the hospital.

It was very bizarre because, from the moment I took the first shot, I never felt any pain. Rather, a peaceful feeling was spreading throughout my body, like I had been injected with a very strong tranquilizer. Everything kept slowing down so much that, as my eyes finally closed, there was only the click-click of frozen frames. Daisy screamed that we were finally at the hospital. I got out to walk to the emergency entrance, immediately experienced a big white flash, then fell to the ground. Several medical personnel rushed out, and they began asking me questions. And then I saw two police uniforms.

Somebody was cutting off my pants, and I started babbling. "Why are you doing that?"

"We're gonna lose him!" somebody kept shouting.

Daisy was nearby, screaming over and over: "Don't close your eyes!"

"Did you get a load of that car?" one of the police officers said.

The other cop was looking down at me. "What did you do?"

The medical team lifted me onto a stretcher and began rolling me toward the emergency entrance.

"Keep still," one of them said to me. "You've lost a lot of blood."

In a few moments I was in the operating room, the strong smell of antiseptic filling my nostrils.

"You're hemorrhaging and have lost a lot of blood," said a doctor with a medical face mask who was hovering over me. "We're going to put you out. Is there anybody you need to call?"

I just wanted to close my eyes. I had no strength, not even to speak one word. Sleep, that's all I wanted. I began to dream I was lost inside a big castle, wandering through its long hallways, wanting to enter and sleep in each room. It was a very relaxing, cozy dream. Suddenly, in a low voice, I heard my name being called. It seemed like the dream had lasted only a few minutes. In fact, I had been out for hours. After hearing my name being repeated several times, I finally opened my eyes.

"Are you okay?" Anthony was standing over me.

"He didn't try to rob me. I have all MT's stuff."

"Man, what you thinking? You've been shot." Anthony was shaking his head disapprovingly, indicating that I had my priorities very messed up. "Hey," he added, "there's somebody here to see you."

As he approached the side of my bed dressed in sweat pants and a jacket, Mike Tyson looked disoriented.

"I found the keys, Rudy," he said softly. MT was talking about the keys to the Diablo which I had left back at the house before Anthony took me to the airport. Sometime ago I had mentioned to my boss that, if I wasn't going to be around for awhile, I would leave the keys to the cars in a place he wouldn't easily forget, the cookie jar in the kitchen which he frequently checked out. Shortly after midnight, when they learned what had happened to me in Los Angeles, Mike Tyson and Anthony Pitts bolted out of the Vegas house, jumped into the Diablo, and raced across the desert to be at my side.

"I didn't do nothing wrong," I told my boss. "He didn't take anything."

Don't concern yourself with that." Tyson glanced over at Anthony like "why is he still talking about my stuff when he almost just got killed?"

Out of the corner of my eye I could see that Mike Tyson looked both sad and scared. "You know they're trying to kill you, right?" He gazed down at me in silence for a few moments, then said: "I want you to go straight to the house in Vegas."

Our conversation was over because I passed out. It seemed like only a minute, but actually it was several hours. As daylight streamed in through the window in my room, I experienced massive pain throughout my entire body, even in my toes. My back and shoulders felt like somebody was sticking needles in them. As I lay there waiting for a doctor or nurse, I had no idea whether I was going to be crippled as a result of the injuries that I had sustained in the shooting. Anthony was trying to make arrangements to get me released, but he was encountering resistance. Finally, against the attending physician's advice, and after I agreed to release the hospital from any liability, I was discharged.

During my operation, the doctors fitted me with an artificial artery. Wrapped in bandages, still bleeding, and in massive pain, Anthony took me to the airport where we caught a plane to Vegas. Tyson had made arrangements for me to be admitted to a hospital, but Anthony instructed the taxi driver to take us to another address. We arrived at my boss's house. Anthony opened the door for me, and inside I could see King, Holloway, Horne, and their wives. Mike

Tyson then appeared and walked up to me slowly.

"Are you okay?" he asked quietly, a glazed look on his face like he had been drugged.

King, Horne, and Holloway turned around. It was obvious they were shocked to see me standing there.

"What were you doing with my Rolls?" Don King blurted out. "What were you doing in California?"

Don King denied that he had told Dana Jamison to send me on the errand to pick up his Bentley. Mike Tyson was staring at King and Holloway. John Horne had turned away so that Tyson wouldn't be able to see his face.

"You're stupid!" Horne said. "You should've given up the car. Why did you get shot up? It had insurance."

Before I could respond, Mike Tyson fixed his gaze on John Horne. "They didn't wanna rob him. He didn't get shot at over that. Why don't you stop playing games? You niggers are trying to kill him because of the checks."

There was a stunned silence in the room for a few moments. Then they all looked at Mike Tyson like he had made the joke of the century and started chuckling. But Tyson's expression remained dead serious. He instructed Anthony to take me to the Lake Mead Hospital Medical Center. When we arrived, the doctors were standing by to perform my next surgery. That same week I had another surgery. For a time there was concern the path a bullet had created might paralyze my arm from the elbow down. Refusing to accept such a fate, I went over and over in my mind that I was going to be okay. I was very fortunate and eventually regained most of the mobility in the arm which gunshots had ripped apart.

Because I needed total rest during my recuperation, I

wasn't able to attend the June 28, 1991 Tyson-Ruddock rematch. Just like the first fight, it was held at The Mirage's outdoor arena. I watched the bout on television from my hospital room. For the first time in four years, Mike Tyson was forced to go the entire twelve rounds before being declared the winner by unanimous decision. The last time he had to fight twelve rounds was on August 1, 1987 at the Las Vegas Hilton when he won by unanimous decision against Tony Tucker. Tyson's punches were good enough to break a bone in Ruddock's jaw but not good enough to knock him out in MT's signature early-finish style. In fact, as Tyson struggled to put the big Jamaican away, the crowd turned on him and began cheering the embattled Ruddock in the closing rounds.

Although his record stood at 41-1, with thirty-six knockouts, "Iron Mike" Tyson still wasn't the heavyweight champion. To achieve that goal, he would have to go up against Evander "The Real Deal" Holyfield, something MT had been insisting on for months. And now, with the Razor Ruddock controversy finally put to rest, everybody was waiting for that date to be set. Don King began his efforts to sandbag that event from happening as soon as Tyson-Ruddock II had ended.

"He has proven he is bigger than the title! He is bigger than any fighter in the world. You're talking about a symbol." By this Don King tried to create the illusion there wasn't any reason for Tyson to fight Holyfield because the heavyweight title was just "ceremonial."

"You wonder how long King can continue selling this frayed bill of goods to Tyson," a reporter wrote in the *Los Angeles Daily News* two days after Tyson-Ruddock II. "You wonder how King can keep Tyson focused on the Nov. 1 fight with Foreman he is proposing. You wonder when Tyson will end the charade, look King in the eye, and say enough is enough: 'My next fight will be with Holyfield for the title, and it will take place with or without you.' You wonder if King is scared to death."

Evander Holyfield's promoter, Dan Duva, offered Tyson $15 million for a chance at the title, but Don King claimed the rival promoter was demanding terms which were unfavorable to Tyson. King wanted $25 million for Tyson's participation. He also said Duva had demanded options for future Mike Tyson fights on *TVKO*, *HBO*'s pay-per-view network. However, the network's president, Seth Abraham, denied that such a demand had been made a condition for setting up the Tyson-Holyfield fight.

"There are two opponents out there we want, Holyfield and Foreman," Don King said. "And the way things are now, whichever one signs first with us will be the one we go with." King offered to pay George Foreman $15 million, plus a percentage of the pay-per-view revenue from *KingVision/Showtime*, if he agreed to fight Mike Tyson on November 1, 1991 at The Mirage.

"King doesn't want Tyson to fight Holyfield," Dan Duva observed, "because if Tyson loses, King won't have any influence in the heavyweight division."

Shortly after being discharged from the Lake Mead Hospital Medical Center, Don King's secretary told me that two detectives from the Los Angeles Police Department wanted to speak with me about the shooting. They showed me photos of some suspects, but I didn't recognize any of those individuals. The detectives said that they would get in touch with me again, but they never did.

The day after Tyson-Ruddock II, my boss asked me to return with him to The Big House in Southington, Ohio, located about fifty miles southeast of Cleveland in Amish country. He spent most of his time there just hanging out doing nothing. MT's impatience was growing to a fever pitch while he waited for Don King to set up the Evander Holyfield title match. Mike Tyson was determined to be the world heavyweight champion again by the end of 1991, regardless whether King was working to make that happen. In fact, MT had been out of control for some time already, a loose cannon, doing things on his own which had been pissing Don King off to no end.

For example, on December 28, 1990, about eleven months after the Buster Douglas fiasco in Japan, Mike Tyson filed a $50 million lawsuit to stop the heavyweight match between Evander Holyfield and George Foreman set for April 19, 1991 in Atlantic City. The suit was filed in federal court in Manhattan against the World Boxing Association and the International Boxing Federation. The other major boxing organization, the World Boxing Council, had ruled that Tyson should fight Holyfield for the title. In his complaint, Tyson alleged that he should have been allowed to fight Holyfield, the winner against Buster Douglas in a fight held two months before at The Mirage. Tyson also claimed that Holyfield wanted to fight Foreman because he would be easier to beat.

The relief Tyson was seeking in that legal action directly conflicted with Don King's game plan for staging a series of Tyson "road to recovery" matches designed to rake in millions for Don King Productions. By July, 1991, there already had been four such "recovery" fights, against opponents Tillman, Stewart, and then Ruddock twice. For Mike Tyson, all this posturing made absolutely no sense. It was not about the money. Instead, it was about who was the best heavyweight fighter in the world. And in July of 1991, just as it had been in December of 1990, that issue could only be decided by Mike Tyson fighting the current heavyweight titleholder, "Real Deal" Holyfield. It made no difference to Mike Tyson whether that fight would be held at Caesars Palace or in an alley down the street.

Mike Tyson also was waiting for Don King to give him answers about his financial situation and what had happened to me in Los Angeles. No response had been provided yet about the Genesis Motorcoach deposit nor the money Mike Tyson Productions was paying for Don King Production expenses. My boss also had given the word that John Horne and Rory Holloway were not to be hanging around him constantly like they had been ever since Don King had taken over his business affairs.

There always had been girls around Tyson because he had an incredible sexual appetite. However, during this time after the Ruddock rematch, MT spent more quiet time at The Big House thinking about what had been happening in his life in the recent past. My boss had some local girlfriends who would pass by from time to time, but MT spent more time just watching cartoons and ninja movies.

On the night of July 17, 1991, Tyson was sleeping upstairs after entertaining a few friends visiting from Los Angeles. The phone rang around midnight. It was the mother of Demencio, a close childhood friend from Mike Tyson's days in the old Brooklyn neighborhood. She was calling from Washington, DC where the family had moved awhile back. Over the years, Demencio had kept in close touch with MT and had attended most of his fights. Demencio's mother informed me that earlier that day her son had been shot to death. The reason for the killing still was a mystery. I went upstairs and told my boss about the death of his friend. He picked up the phone and began consoling Demencio's mother, and I went back downstairs.

A few minutes later a very upset Tyson descended the stairs and breezed right past me. I heard the distinct roar of the Porsche 911 Speedster, the fastest car in my boss's collection, heading down the driveway. The security guard called and asked what to do. "Open the gates!" I yelled out, then dialed Ouie's number in New York.

"Lock down the house, Rudy," Ouie instructed me. "Go after MT. Don't let him go to DC. There might be some type of war going on there, and they might retaliate against MT."

I quickly rounded up the staff and told them to leave immediately because we were shutting down The Big House. Only Maria, the chef, was to remain there.

***

By the time I got everything organized and was able to leave the house, Tyson had more than an hour's jump on me. I grabbed a few personal items, tossed them in the black Ferrari Testarossa, and headed east on I-80, driving like a maniac in search of my boss. I finally saw MT in the distance being chased by the Pennsylvania State Police. I clocked Tyson doing around 160 miles per hour. I didn't want to lose them, but I didn't want to get stopped either so I slowed down. A few minutes later, I was able to catch up to Tyson, but only because the state troopers finally had been able to pull him over.

They were about to arrest him when I approached one of the troopers, a towering black man. I identified myself as Mike Tyson's bodyguard and said I had been looking for him. I told the trooper one of Tyson's best friends had been killed in DC, that he was very emotional and upset, and that he was tying to get there to learn what had happened. The trooper said he had to give my boss a speeding ticket because he already had printed it out, but he agreed not to arrest him. However, in addition to receiving the citation, Tyson would have to leave the Porsche at a nearby service station and continue on with me. The troopers considered my boss a menace to himself and others in light of his current emotional state. They escorted us to the service station to make sure we followed their orders.

After we parked and locked the Porsche, Tyson jumped into the Testarossa, and we headed for DC. It was a seven-hour drive, but we did it in four, arriving in the Capital in the early morning. We went to the apartment of a long-standing Tyson girlfriend, Sherry Brown, located in a poor section of town. I stayed with the car while MT went inside. During the entire trip my boss had been very upset and agitated. I was so exhausted that I fell asleep, awakened sometime later by my Skypager. The number was that of The Big House in Southington. I glanced at my watch and saw it was nearly 9 a.m. I called the number expecting our chef, Maria, to answer. Instead, Don King's voice came over the line.

"Goddammit, where's Mike?" he shouted. "Where are you fucking guys now?! I need to talk to Mike."

"DK, one of his friends got killed last night. We just got into DC this morning, and he's upstairs sleeping in Sherry's apartment."

"I've gotta talk to that nigger right now!"

"Sir, I'll give him the message," I said and hung up.

After locking the car, I went inside Sherry Brown's building. MT was passed out on the couch. I placed my hand on his shoulder in a special way which was a sign to him that it was me. You just didn't tap Mike Tyson on the arm or head because he could wake up swinging. For this reason, I was the only one who ever woke him up. Even Robin Givens used to tell me to wake her husband up. It was too dangerous.

"Hey, boss. Don King wants to talk to you."

"I don't wanna talk to nobody, man" he said, rolling over, his eyes still closed.

Back inside the Testarossa I fell asleep again until another page awakened me. When I called The Big House, this time both Don King and John Horne were on the line, screaming and demanding to speak with Mike Tyson.

"Goddammit, Rudy, Mike will speak to me!" King kept shouting.

Back inside Sherry Brown's apartment, MT got on the phone with Don King. It apparently had to do with King insisting that Tyson go somewhere immediately. But my boss kept telling King he didn't want to go, that he wasn't "in the mood," and that he "didn't need to do that." The conversation went back and forth like that for awhile. Then, as always, Mike Tyson gave in and agreed to do whatever it was that Don King had demanded he do.

"All right, all right! I'll go, I'll go. Just get off my shit, man. Just book us on the next flight." MT hung up and turned to me. "We've got to go to fucking Indianapolis."

I couldn't believe it. Here we were in DC to spend some time with the family of a close Tyson childhood friend who had just been killed. We had driven for hours at race-car speeds to get here, and now, in the early morning, King ordered us to catch a plane to Indianapolis on a moment's notice. King made Tyson cave in by laying a guilt trip on him: he had to make a personal appearance in Indianapolis for the sake of America's black youth.

"Look, Rudy, the motherfucker promised the black children of Indiana I'll be at this Black Expo thing. We'll fly in, spend the day, and B Angie B will be there. I'll dip in a little sauce, and we'll be outta there. It ain't no thing."

Sherry Brown agreed to say her goodbyes at the airport and followed us out to Washington National in her Jaguar, a gift from MT. Tyson smooched with Sherry while I headed for the long-term parking garage. When I got back, they were hugging for the last time, and then Brown climbed into the Jaguar and sped away. We walked over to the USAir counter where they were holding two first-class tickets for us on the 11 a.m. flight to Indianapolis. As we approached the gate, I recognized a fat, greasy-looking guy waiting to board the same flight. I couldn't believe it! The man was Dale Edwards, one of Don King's nephews.

"Yo, big D, what the fuck you doing here?" I asked.

"I'm escorting Mike Tyson to Indianapolis," he said, as if we already knew. "DK wanted to make sure I was with him today. We'll meet everybody in Indianapolis."

Something definitely was very wrong with this picture. It made absolutely no sense Dale Edwards was in DC to "escort" Mike Tyson. That had been my job almost every day of my life since May of 1987. King knew I was with Tyson because I had spoken with him earlier that day. Dale Edwards never had been responsible for guarding Tyson. He wasn't bonded, meaning my boss wouldn't have any insurance coverage if there were an incident. At that moment, the flight was called so we all boarded the plane. My boss settled in and turned on his Walkman. A moment later, a flight attendant approached me.

"Mr. Gonzalez?" she asked, and I nodded. "The ticket agent needs to speak with you."

"Is there a problem?"

"Sir, I really don't know, but you do need to depart the aircraft and see the ticket agent."

I tapped MT's arm, and he removed the earphones. I told him there was a problem with my ticket. "Come on, get off with me." I didn't want to let him out of my sight the way things had been going these days.

"No, man, you just take care of it yourself." Tyson was mourning the death of a close friend and didn't want to be bothered at the time. He put the earphones back on and closed his eyes.

Cursing under my breath, I walked quickly through the jetway and then rushed over to the VIP ticket counter. There a lady informed me that my ticket had been voided.

"Contact Don King Productions. There's gotta be a mistake," I said impatiently.

"Sir, you're going to have to do that yourself." She pointed me in the direction of a courtesy phone. I dialed DKP and spoke to the receptionist who put me through to Don King who already had returned to New York.

"Yo, Don, what's the problem? We're here. We're ready to get on the flight. My ticket's been cancelled."

Don King put the call on speakerphone, and I could hear John Horne in the background. "You ain't goin' on that goddamn flight!" King shouted. "Now get your ass in the Ferrari, drive it to Ohio, and leave Mike alone."

"Anthony's on the way from LA to meet MT in Indianapolis," Horne added. "So do what the fuck Don tells you do to!"

As I slammed the phone down, Tyson's airplane pulled away from the gate. "Fuck!" I yelled out, grabbed the phone again, and paged Ouie. A few minutes later, the courtesy phone rang.

"Ouie, something's wrong. MT's alone." I told him about the series of events which had led us to the airport. We decided the best thing to do was for me to go to New York so, against Don King's orders, I raced the Testarossa to the City. In the early afternoon I pulled up to Don King Productions on East 69th Street. The staff said they didn't know where King was, but I insisted they keep trying to locate him, Horne, and Holloway. They grudgingly made some calls, but all three apparently were incommunicado. I paged Horne and Holloway myself, but I didn't get a response from either of them.

My head was throbbing from all the bullshit which had been going on and all the games which were being played. This type of scenario never had happened before. I should have been with my boss on that July 18, 1991 flight, then by his side at all times in Indianapolis, including at his hotel during the early morning hours of the next day.

Before heading back to The Big House in Ohio, I

stopped by my Mother's apartment in Spanish Harlem where I visited with her and some friends for about an hour. Around 9 p.m. I arrived at the Southington property. I asked the security guard to drive me back to the airport so I could catch a flight to DC. I got there around midnight, then took a taxi to the Pennsylvania service station where the highway patrol officers had ordered Tyson to leave his Porsche 911 Speedster. After paying the very large cab fare, I climbed into the Porsche and headed northwest to Southington. I drove most of the night, stopping only a few times at service areas for short naps. It was the first time in recent memory where I respected the speed limits. Around 6 a.m. I reentered the grounds of The Big House.

Mike Tyson called around 7 a.m. and said he would be arriving in Cleveland at 8:40 a.m. He told me to pick him up there so, without showering or shaving, I drove to Cleveland Hopkins International. Because there was no place to park at the airport, I waited for him curbside. When Tyson exited the terminal, he was accompanied by Dale Edwards who continued on to the long-term parking lot where he had left his car. Before I was forced to depart the Washington to Indianapolis flight, as a result of my ticket being cancelled, I had left a leather clutch with my boss. It contained $10,000 and four condoms. I took a look at the clutch and mentioned to MT that $4,000 and two condoms were missing from it.

"Who you been fucking with?" I asked him. At this point in time, I was concerned with MT's sexual behavior. Long before he revealed it to the world, Magic Johnson called a meeting with Mike Tyson and Arsenio Hall, two of his closest friends, to let them know he had been diagnosed

HIV positive. Magic Johnson and Mike Tyson had shared many of the same groupies. Therefore, two things became very important for me after that meeting: keeping track of all the girls with whom my boss had sexual relations and making sure he used condoms with them.

"I didn't spend no $4,000," MT mumbled, shaking his head. "No fucking way, man. I don't know what the fuck happened to it."

"What about the two rubbers?"

Tyson told me that he had used them for sex with rapper B Angie B and another girl. On the way back to The Big House, MT said he was very tired and wanted to crash. He didn't want any noise disturbing him. I hit the sack until 2 p.m., then went to where chef Maria was making lunch. My boss was snoring away upstairs. I went back to sleep until around 5 p.m. when Maria woke me up. She said there was a young lady on the phone who wanted to speak with Mr. Tyson. I informed her that MT was not to be bothered under any circumstances, but Maria already knew that. The problem was this girl kept insisting that she be put through to Mike Tyson.

"I'll take the call in my room," I told the chef. A moment later I punched the flashing hold button.

"I want to talk to Mike Tyson."

"He's not available."

"Who's this?"

"This is his personal aide. What can I do for you?"

"I need to talk to Mike."

"What's your name?"

"This is Desiree Washington."

At first I thought it was "Desree," a Tyson girlfriend

who lived in DC. When I asked about the weather there, I realized that I had made a mistake.

"You must have me confused with somebody else," she said, her voice much colder now. "This is the Desiree Washington. He met me yesterday."

"He's sleeping now. Leave me a message, and I'll make sure he gets back to you."

"I'll call him back," she said and hung up.

I went back to sleep until around 8 p.m. Later that night I was in the kitchen when the phone rang. MT was still upstairs resting.

"Mr. Tyson's residence. May I help you?"

I recognized the same voice that I had heard earlier in the day. "I want to speak with Mike Tyson."

Her tone revealed that she had a big attitude.

"This is Rudy again," I told her. "Mr. Tyson still is not available."

"I need to speak with him now."

"He doesn't want to be disturbed right now."

"When is he going to call me back?" It was clear this young lady was very annoyed at being put off.

"I really don't know, miss. He has many priority messages to return."

I now was certain that my boss must have just met her. She didn't understand the rules of the celebrity game. Unless you were a very important person, you took a place in line like everybody else.

"If you'll just be patient, I'm sure that he'll get back to you."

"Listen," she snapped, "Mike Tyson better talk to me now. It's better sooner than later." Then she hung up.

That was the second and only other time I ever spoke to Desiree Washington. Later I would think how incredibly ironic it was that Don King had ordered Mike Tyson to get on an airplane in Washington and travel to a place where he would end up meeting Washington.

***

Not long after I got off the phone with Desiree Washington, Tyson came downstairs looking for food. In the meantime, I had spoken to Anthony Pitts to catch up on things. He still was in Los Angeles. Anthony didn't go to Indianapolis because John Horne told him there was no need to interrupt his honeymoon and travel halfway across the country when I was going to be with MT anyway. When Tyson entered the kitchen, I told him that me and Anthony were very pissed that we had been lied to.

"We'll deal with that shit later. Let me eat, man."

"A bitch, Desiree Washington, has been calling you. What's up with her? She seems to have a problem."

My boss's eyes widened. "I don't wanna talk to her. She was playing games with me in the hotel."

After they had done "the wild thing," she "freaked out." Desiree Washington had been upset because Tyson didn't escort her downstairs to the limousine waiting to take her back to her own hotel. But Tyson never escorted anyone down from an apartment or hotel room after sex. He left that for his bodyguards to do.

"Why did you let Don King take me off the plane? Me or Anthony should've been with you."

Tyson just shrugged off my question. "Listen, we're going to bury Demencio in Brooklyn. Pull out a black suit and get ready to fly to New York."

That same evening, July 19, 1991, we received two crank calls at The Big House. The next morning we caught an early flight to New York to attend Demencio's funeral. After the burial the following day, MT went to dinner with a group of friends from the old days. He tried his best to cheer everybody up, wanting them to remember Demencio as someone who had made them laugh over the years.

Don King had been trying to reach Tyson, but my boss didn't want to speak with him. King wanted to talk about the fact that Tyson was dealing directly with Caesars Palace to schedule a fight with Evander "The Real Deal" Holyfield. We were driving around with Anthony Pitts and Sherry Brown when MT suddenly told me to take them to King's townhouse. He had decided he was going to talk to Don King about the Holyfield fight. We were greeted by the maid, and Tyson asked her about getting some buffalo wings. She then showed us to the living room and turned on the television. We were just hanging out trading jokes when a news bulletin came on.

"On July 19, former heavyweight champion, Mike Tyson, is alleged to have raped a beauty contestant, Desiree Washington, at the Black Expo in Indianapolis."

All of us were in shock except for Mike Tyson. Instead, he looked very disappointed, like someone whom he had trusted had let him down. Desiree Washington had never run to a hospital, the police, or anyone else after that early-morning encounter with Mike Tyson in Room 606 at the Canterbury Hotel. In fact, she had called The Big House twice during the afternoon of that same day wanting to speak with my boss. I was the one who had answered the phone and taken her messages on those two occasions. MT never called her back that day. Desiree Washington waited until the following day before she decided to report to the authorities that she had been raped by Mike Tyson.

After a few moments, MT said in a low voice. "I can't understand why they're doing this to me."

We sat there in silence not knowing what to say. A few moments later, Don King arrived at the townhouse and strolled into the living room. He took off his leather jacket and threw it on a table.

"Now you need my help, nigger!" He boomed in Tyson's direction. "Your dick got you in trouble now! Goddammit, Mike, now you need me!"

Mike Tyson didn't say anything. He just lowered his head as if he were a small child being scolded.

***

Don King started taking over even more of Mike Tyson's affairs, including his defense against the criminal charges in the Desiree Washington case. On September 9, 1991, a grand jury in Marion County, Indiana handed down an indictment charging Tyson with one count of rape, two counts of deviate sexual conduct, and one count of confinement. He entered a plea of "not guilty" to each count, asserting the encounter between him and Washington involved consensual sex. To represent Tyson, King hired Vincent J. Fuller, a sixty-year-old attorney from the DC law firm of Williams and Connolly. Fuller had represented King before. Now that lawyer was given the task of defending Tyson in the trial set for January 27, 1992 in Indianapolis.

In October of 1991, we were in New York City staying at Tyson's new condo unit near the United Nations. We were going out that night and had planned on using the

Lamborghini SUV. However, it had a flat tire, and we were unable to change it. You needed four guys to perform that task on this three-ton exotic truck. I mentioned that there was a Mercedes 500 SEL parked at The Churchill, Celia Tuckman's building. We had discovered that my boss was paying for her residence even though she didn't work for Mike Tyson Productions. Tuckman was the executive vice-president of Don King Productions. This Mercedes was listed as a "corporate vehicle" for the Mike Tyson Fan Club, an entity wholly-owned by Don King's family. MT ordered me to retrieve the Mercedes 500 SEL so I grabbed a taxi and went to The Churchill.

This vehicle was very beautiful with a brilliant white exterior and plush blue interior, spoiler kit, and 16" wheels. The name "Don King" was engraved on the seats. That night MT and some of his close buddies were drinking champagne. While we were driving around Mike Tyson suddenly got angry. He turned to me and said: "Fuck this shit up." I didn't understand what he meant so my boss explained he wanted me to start smashing up this vehicle, a demolition derby, using any objects I could find. At around 3 a.m., on Lexington Avenue, I began slamming the Mercedes into parking meters. I'll never forget the stunned look we got from The Churchill parking attendant. The next day we learned that Don King and Celia Tuckman had gone ballistic when they inspected what was left of the Mercedes 500 SEL in Celia Tuckman's parking space.

Mike Tyson returned to Las Vegas to train for the bout with Evander Holyfield scheduled for November 8, 1991 at Caesars Palace. About a month before the fight was to take place, my boss was injured under very suspicious circumstances. John Horne showed up at the gym with some gravity boots. "Back up," he said to Richie Giachetti. "I'm training Mike this afternoon." Horne told the trainer they needed to work on Tyson's abdominals because Holyfield was a "stomach puncher." Giachetti had been using his own proven techniques to get Tyson into top fighting condition, but there always seemed to be interference with his efforts.

"What the fuck do you know about training?" a very frustrated Giachetti asked Horne. "You ain't no trainer." Richie Giachetti then walked out of the gym.

John Horne knew less about boxing than I knew about nuclear physics. Aaron Snowell and Carl King also were present at the training session. They helped slip the gravity boots onto MT's feet, and then hung him upside down on a bar. Tyson never had used this training method before. He started doing sit-ups and, after about 100 of them, on an upward swing we heard a pop. Tyson had torn a cartilage in his rib cage, but this was not an injury serious enough to prevent him from fighting anybody on the planet, including Evander Holyfield, a month down the road. Even if Mike Tyson had three broken ribs and a hangover, he still could knock "The Real Deal" Holyfield on his ass within a few seconds. However, this minor injury was a true godsend for Don King who immediately announced to the world his fighter was out of commission, requiring that the match with Holyfield be cancelled.

When Mike Tyson heard this, he was enraged. But he had to contend with the rape trial in Indianapolis, which was just around the corner, and Don King was running that show. The time was not ripe for an ugly confrontation with the man taking care of his defense in that very serious criminal case. *The Miami Herald* reported that the Tyson-Holyfield fight was expected to be "the first $100 million bout, and its postponement may still set a new mark—the most expensive party never thrown...The trial means that the party might never happen."

We returned to The Big House in Southington, Ohio. Soon Mike Tyson's life would take a final nosedive into the toilet while Don King kept telling him there was no way a jury was going to convict him in Indianapolis. MT started hanging out with a guy called Iceberg Slim, a well-known former pimp with some very bad habits. Don King and John Horne had introduced Iceberg Slim to Tyson. A lot of low-life characters started hanging around The Big House during this period. They encouraged MT to engage in offensive behavior and act like an idiot instead of preparing for the upcoming trial. Don King, Iceberg Slim, and others also started laying a new rap on my boss: his criminal charges were the "white man's fault." Mike Tyson was turning increasingly angrier at everybody and everything in the world.

During the spring of 1991, the luxury automobiles comprising Mike Tyson's inventory, numbering around one hundred, needed their registrations renewed. It turned out they were being re-registered in the name of The Mike Tyson Fan Club in Orwell, Ohio, a corporation wholly-owned and operated by Don King Productions. Debbie King, Don King's daughter, was its vice-president. The $2,000 check made out to her, which we discovered that watershed day of June 12, 1991 in Mike Tyson's Las Vegas bedroom, was to pay her salary. I remembered Henrietta King, Don King's wife, had signed Tyson's name on the renewal forms for these cars. Again, my Panasonic scanner came in very handy to document what was going on.

Before his trial began in Indianapolis, Mike Tyson met with Vince Fuller, his defense attorney, a total of two times. The first meeting was back in September, shortly after the indictment was returned, and it lasted barely ten minutes. Don King, Anthony Pitts, and John Horne were there. Because Fuller seemed concerned only with what Mike Tyson was going to wear at trial, I decided to speak up. I told the attorney that on July 20 Desiree Washington had called The Big House twice. It was easy to see that Vince Fuller did not know this critical fact because his expression was one of shock.

Don King jumped out of his chair. "That's bullshit! Don't believe him!"

"He's right, Don," Tyson said, confirming the truth of what I had just told Fuller.

"Goddammit, Rudy, don't ever say that shit again! It ain't got nothing to do with this so just keep your motherfucking mouth shut!"

Anthony Pitts turned to Tyson. "Why don't we just say we were with you, MT?"

John Horne began yelling. "Shut the fuck up! Stop bullshitting!"

Don King started talking about William Kennedy Smith who had been charged in a very high-profile rape case in Palm Beach, Florida. King assured Tyson that he didn't have to worry about losing. "You'll get off. Don't listen to those crazy motherfuckers."

During this entire exchange, Vince Fuller never said a word. By the time we left Williams & Connolly that day, Don King and John Horne had convinced Tyson that, in the worst-case scenario, he would get nothing more than a slap on the wrist. We returned to The Big House in Southington where Mike Tyson's anti-social behavior continued to spiral downward under the watchful eyes of Don King associates, like Iceberg Slim, who systematically were dragging my boss through the gutter. As MT's trial date rapidly approached, I thought about getting a new legal team to work with him. My boss needed to start preparing for trial because there was no preparation going on between him and his current defense attorney. We had traveled to DC several times between September 1991 and January 1992. However, only Don King and John Horne met with Vince Fuller on those occasions. Horne instructed me and Anthony "not to bother MT anymore" about the case because there would be no problem. During those trips MT and I usually just hung around outside the Williams & Connolly building talking to girls while the others were inside with Vince Fuller.

For the second and only other trip where he actually met with Vince Fuller to prepare his defense, MT flew to DC with Don King. I drove the Lincoln-Continental limo with passengers Anthony Pitts, Isadore Bolton, and a Don King relative named Craig whose main role was to procure women and organize group sex. Craig also was responsible for taking videos while he and others encouraged Tyson to act obnoxious on camera. The night before my boss flew to DC, with the possibility that he might lose the case now finally sinking in, he gave me final instructions. I packed the limo with several trunks of Tyson's clothing, approximately $1.3 million in cash, and what certainly was several million more of his diamond and gold jewelry.

"Collect everything," MT told me as we emptied his

safe in The Big House. "I want you to take care of my business. I don't want any of those niggers in my house. Don't let anybody fuck with my shit." He was referring to Don King, John Horne, Rory Holloway, and their intimates who had been leeching themselves off the Mike Tyson money machine for so long.

"Rudy, I've never taken care of you," he said as he finished gathering up the last of his things. "You've got one big one coming." By that Mike Tyson meant that he was going to give me a million dollars.

When I didn't respond, Mike Tyson turned around and found me standing at attention, just like I had done a thousand times before. Even when his world might soon come to an end, even when he was the most vulnerable, entrusting me and nobody else with the most important details of his life, I was still acting as respectfully and professionally as I had when I first became his servant one very cold early November morning in 1986.

"Rudy, if anything happens to me, just take care of your shit."

Looking at his face for what would be the last time before his rape trial started, it seemed to me that Mike Tyson had convinced himself, during these last moments in the master bedroom of The Big House in Southington, Ohio, that powerful forces around him were going to take him out of the picture regardless of the truth.

"The Final Round"

"The Final Round"

On January 25, 1992, a very cold but cloudless day, I pulled the Lincoln-Continental limo up to the entrance of The Capital Hilton in northwest Washington. Mike Tyson already was in DC meeting with Vince Fuller at Williams & Connolly. It was just two days before MT's rape trial was scheduled to begin in Indianapolis. John Horne was ready to pounce on us the moment we arrived at the hotel.

"Come over here!" Horne ordered all of us, tilting his head in the direction of the lobby.

I grabbed the Louis Vuitton vanity case containing millions of dollars of Tyson's jewelry and entered the hotel.

"Anthony, MT wants you to go back to California until this is all over," Horne instructed Pitts. "Then you're back on the team. Isadore, you go up and start unpacking everything. And now," Horne said, turning to me with his trademark weasel smile and an outstretched hand. "It's your turn. Hand over the safe box with all the jewelry."

When I didn't comply, Horne began yelling: "Hand over the box, hand over the box!"

Don King appeared at Horne's side. "Goddammit, take the fucking jewelry from him. I'm tired of this shit!"

There was no way I was going to deliver millions of my boss's jewelry to these two jerks so I demanded to see Mike Tyson. But King and Horne refused and continued to verbally threaten me. Their body language signaled that they might try and pounce on me at any moment. I decided to pull out the company's 9mm Glock pistol to prevent this, keeping it at my side instead of pointing it in their direction. At that moment several Secret Service agents came out of nowhere and bolted toward me. Apparently, they were there to protect political figures and be on the lookout for behavior which might constitute a danger to them.

After I produced credentials proving that I worked for Mike Tyson Productions, the DC police were called in. I explained to the officers that there were millions of dollars of Tyson's personal property in my custody, and I was not going to release it to anyone except my boss. Don King denied he had tried to take possession of the property and quickly disappeared from the lobby. John Horne told the police he worked for Tyson, and there would be no problem as long as I agreed to release the property to him.

Because I had credentials and was wearing a Team Tyson jacket, the cops believed I had certain authority over this property. However, they needed instructions directly from MT about how to resolve this dispute and sent someone to meet with him. A few minutes later, Rory Holloway came down to the lobby with the settlement proposal. MT's valuables would be placed in the hotel safe, and I would have to surrender the 9mm Glock pistol. Two of the officers recommended that I give up the firearm. With my boss under indictment, and possibly soon a convicted felon, Mike Tyson Productions probably wouldn't be bondable. Any problems arising over my carrying this handgun could cause the company some legal problems.

John Horne confronted me one more time as I was

about to leave The Capital Hilton. "Give me the fucking computer, Rudy."

"Fuck you, I ain't giving you shit!"

"Give me the fucking computer you're always writing in," Horne demanded again.

A lot of people knew about the Sharp "Wizard," a wallet-sized device I always carried with me. They saw me constantly tapping away, entering or retrieving information. I had been using the Wizard, not just as a phone directory and appointment calendar, but also as a log of important events in Mike Tyson's life. Those events included his sexual encounters, and whether he had used a condom. The device also was used to keep track of MT's automobile collection as well as the jewelry my boss had given as gifts to his numerous one-night stands I also had stored in the Sharp Wizard information about the many confrontations with Don King. John Horne needed this device to get his hands on all this information so he could turn it over to King, his master and benefactor.

"I ain't giving you my fucking computer."

"Give me the fucking computer!"

I turned around and noticed the local police still lingering around the hotel lobby. I figured this issue was going to end up being resolved the same way as Tyson's personal property. So I pulled the Sharp Wizard from my shirt pocket and pressed the reset button which wiped out the master memory. I ejected the disc and slipped it into my shirt pocket. Turning back to Horne, I handed him the device which no longer contained any information. John Horne never had a clue.

I boarded a Trump Shuttle and flew to LaGuardia

Airport. I stayed at my Mother's place in Spanish Harlem for a few days. Mike Tyson's trial began on January 27, 1992, and I followed its progress. On February 10, the jury returned a verdict of guilty on all counts. It was the end of my world. Two days after Tyson's trial had ended, I used some of my savings and headed back to Brazil. I felt like I had to travel thousands of miles to another country to be able to clear my head.

I went over everything that had happened to Mike Tyson during the years I worked for him. Many powerful forces had come into the picture and had worked against his best interests. In the aftermath of the trial, a number of people were speaking out, and numerous articles were being published, criticizing the handling of his defense. Well-known boxing figure Ferdie Pacheco wrote in *Boxing Illustrated* that "huge errors" had been made by Vince Fuller and his team who reportedly received $2 million to handle the defense. "By conceding that Mike Tyson was a ghetto animal in his opening statement, Fuller was sending the wrong message to the jury: 'Well, maybe he didn't rape this girl, but he sure raped a lot of others.'" Ferdie Pacheco concluded: "Mike Tyson had no chance of a fair trial."

Robert Simels, a high-profile Manhattan criminal defense attorney, was quoted in the February 24, 1992 issue of *Time* magazine that Fuller "was probably not the right choice to bring into Indianapolis. They certainly needed a strong local female counsel. A woman could have handled parts of the examination—the questions about panty shields—which are much more sensitive for a male attorney to be hitting a proposed rape victim with." He described other "defense blunders," such as permitting MT to testify to the grand jury, then "allowing Mike to come up with a different story during the trial." This mistake made Mike Tyson look like a liar, and a very bad one at that, "fulfilling any juror's suspicions about the boxer's brutality." The *Time* article made several observations, including that women didn't come to Tyson to "tame the beast" but rather "to unleash him...It's possible that at 2 a.m. on July 19 in Room 606 at the Canterbury Hotel, Tyson was as astonished by Washington's reaction as she was by his action. Tyson runs with the wrong crowd. Many of his friends are paid help, hired as extra muscle or procurers. Don King, the convicted killer who promotes Tyson's bouts, is a sneaky-smooth fighter in smoke-filled rooms."

Sonja Steptoe, a well-known journalist, in an article entitled "A Damnable Defense," recounted some of Vince Fuller's inexplicable strategies. Fuller told the jury that, when Tyson went to Indianapolis after having just won a bout with Razor Ruddock, that he was anxious to "relax for the first time in weeks." I knew that statement was not true. MT had not been "anxious to relax" at the Indiana Black Expo. Instead, he wanted to stay with Demencio's mother in Washington when we received that fateful call from Don King demanding that MT travel to Indianapolis.

In his opening statement, Vince Fuller said to the jury: "I want...you to understand how Mr. Tyson happens to be here in Indianapolis. He had been invited for several years to come to the Black Expo by The Reverend Williams...He didn't come. This year, by coincidence, in the Black Expo program was a young woman singer by the name of B Angie B...Mr. Tyson has kept track of her engagement schedule in the hopes that he'll be able to follow along with her and visit with her as she moves through the country... So now he's relaxing for the first time in weeks...He arranges with B Angie B to meet her in Indianapolis and arranges further for the both of them to go to Cleveland, Ohio, on the morning of the 19th of July because she is performing in Cleveland, Ohio on the evening of the 19th of July. When he knows he's coming to Indianapolis, he does call The Reverend Williams...to tell him he will be here and would be happy to do what little he can for he Black Expo..." Fuller also stated: "Meanwhile, Mr. Tyson is at his hotel. He's awakened at 4:30 in the morning, dresses, proceeds to the airport where he meets B Angie B, and they fly to Cleveland in a somewhat jovial mood." That's *not* what happened. Tyson was not in a "jovial mood" accompanied by B Angie B when he walked out of the Cleveland terminal building. Rather, my boss was with Dale Edwards, the wannabe "bodyguard" who was in the Canterbury Hotel lobby, instead of MT's room where he should have been, when the "incident" occurred.

Sonja Steptoe also wrote that "during the trial Vince Fuller went to great lengths to elicit testimony" about Mike Tyson's "sex-crazed" conduct toward the beauty-pageant contestants. In effect, Fuller was saying to the jury: "Tyson is your worst nightmare—a vulgar, socially-inept, sex-obsessed black athlete." Steptoe observed that the defense team had attempted to introduce expert testimony about the size of Tyson's penis to explain the vaginal abrasions. That trial tactic later was spoofed on *Saturday Night Live*. Steptoe concluded that Tyson was portrayed by his own lawyer as "a stereotypical savage black man run amok." Describing the Indiana Black Expo opening ceremony, Vince Fuller told the jury: "Interestingly enough, Jesse Jackson was there, and

Jesse Jackson beckons to Mr. Tyson to come over to him at a time he's been talking to Miss Washington. Mr. Tyson utters a vulgarity and indicates: 'I don't want to go spend time with Jesse Jackson. He just wants to preach at me. I don't really want to do that.'" Was that the way for Mike Tyson's lawyer to enhance his client's image, or rather was it something the prosecutor should be highlighting?

I read other articles which discussed Mike Tyson's trial. *The National Law Journal* observed: "Even Mr. Tyson seemed a little put off by Mr. Fuller at first. He began the trial sitting next to him, but later moved between [two other] defense lawyers." Vince Fuller's questioning of Desiree Washington was described as "artless, plodding, and remarkably lacking in style," wrote Dan Carpenter of *The Indianapolis Star*. I learned later that Camille Ewald had attended the trial and had held Mike Tyson's hand during part of the proceedings.

Desiree Washington testified that she met Mike Tyson on July 18 during a rehearsal for the Miss Black America Pageant. The Reverend Williams, a Don King intimate, had taken my boss there. How did it happen that Tyson was videotaped at the rehearsal acting in a manner "disrespectful and offensive" to the contestants? At the trial, this videotape was played to the jury. Wasn't Mike Tyson supposed to be at the Indiana Black Expo fulfilling Don King's commitment to support black children?" At the rehearsal, my boss was directed to hug one of the women, and he embraced Washington, who was positioned close to him. She agreed to go out with Tyson that night and gave him the name of her hotel and room number.

One beauty pageant contestant testified that, when

Mike Tyson walked into the rehearsal, Desiree Washington said: "That's $20 million." There was testimony that she had posed for a photograph in Tyson's lap, remained there longer than the other girls, and had to be "pried off." Madeline Whittington, another contestant, ran into Washington in the ladies room who mentioned that she had agreed to go out with my boss. "Of course I'm going. This is Mike Tyson. He's got a lot of money. He's dumb. You see what Robin Givens got out of him." Contestant Cecilia Alexander overheard Desiree Washington say those things. Tanya St. Claire, another participant, related other comments Washington made, including speculation about the size of Mike Tyson's penis. She talked about wanting to land a man with a lot of money. "Robin Givens had him. I can have him too...he's dumb anyway." Her comments about Mike Tyson being "dumb" were confirmed by contestant Caroline Jones. It was very sad to read about these things Desiree Washington had said about my boss who already had suffered enormous deceit and betrayal before that fateful encounter with her.

If Mike Tyson's behavior had been so outrageous at the beauty pageant rehearsal, why would a "nice girl" agree to his "request?" MT had called Washington at 1:36 a.m. He picked her up soon after that at the Omni Severin in a limo the Indiana Black Expo had provided him. Virginia Foster, the driver, testified that Tyson had "begged" Washington to go with him while he made a brief stop back at his room in the Canterbury Hotel.

Desiree Washington testified that at some point Mike Tyson mentioned something "about a bodyguard." Tyson's "bodyguard" that night was Dale Edwards, Don King's nephew, who mysteriously had appeared at the gate of our USAir flight to Indianapolis. I was kicked off that flight because Don King Productions cancelled my ticket. I had been told that it didn't matter because Anthony Pitts was coming from Los Angeles to be with our boss. However, Anthony had been told he didn't have to go to Indianapolis because I was going to be there with MT. Did Tyson believe that Dale Edwards was going to do what a bodyguard was supposed to do, protect the celebrity from false accusations by being near him at all times? Dale Edwards remained in the Canterbury Hotel lobby while Tyson and Washington went up to Room 606 where the alleged incident took place. Although Dale Edwards had testified before the grand jury, the defense did not call him as a witness. In fact, Dale Edwards was missing in action during Mike Tyson's trial.

MT mentioned to me that part of the "weird thing" about Desiree Washington was that she already seemed to know a lot about his personal life, including his love of pigeons. Gregory Garrison, the lead prosecutor, said in his opening statement Tyson had thrown Washington onto the bed "like a rag doll" while his "massive forearm" held her down. Washington testified the bedspread had been pulled back, then stated: "I glanced over and saw the defendant in his underwear...on the bed. He was just sitting there...I was terrified." Something was very wrong here as well. During the more than five years I had known him, Mike Tyson never had sex on a bed, nor did he sleep on one. If Mike Tyson had committed a sexual assault, it never would have taken place on a bed.

I read the brief renowned attorney Alan Dershowitz filed on behalf of Mike Tyson in his appeal. I learned that one witness, Claudia Jordan, had testified that Washington told her that "the incident occurred on the floor." If Vince Fuller had interviewed me, among other things, he would have learned about Tyson's habit of having sex on the floor. He could have put me on the stand to corroborate Jordan's testimony which contradicted the testimony of Desiree Washington. This would have given additional weight to the argument that Washington had fabricated the story she presented at trial.

When Mike Tyson traveled to Indianapolis on July 18, 1991, he was not wearing underwear. He did not have a change of clothing because we hadn't been scheduled to make any trips. MT never wore regular underwear anyway due to his massive thigh muscles. That day he was wearing a Versace summer suit with a "jock strap" sewn into the pants. The suit was designed for use without underwear which would have been exposed through the sheer silk garment and looked very tacky. I could have provided the jury with these very crucial, material facts. Yet, during all the time they were supposed to be carefully preparing for trial, Mike Tyson's attorneys never were interested in how I could help their client win his case.

There was another very important portion of the appellate brief which caught my attention. Three women, Carla J. Martin, Pamela Lawrence, and Renee Neal, saw Tyson and Washington embracing and kissing in the limo as they arrived at the Canterbury Hotel. "They were all over each other," according to Martin. Neal noticed they were holding hands when they entered the lobby. These witnesses could have directly contradicted Washington's testimony that in the lobby she had walked behind Tyson and did not hold hands with him. Washington told the jury that she had been surprised by Tyson's advances toward her after entering Room 606. Vince Fuller had failed to discover the existence of these eyewitnesses. Instead, these three ladies had come forward themselves. However, due to the late notice, the trial judge prohibited the defense from putting them on the stand. Consequently, the jurors never had the benefit of this very favorable evidence.

With a two-million dollar budget, why hadn't Vince Fuller's defense team been able to learn about these three eyewitnesses during all those months before trial? They had been present when Tyson and Washington arrived at the Canterbury Hotel. These three ladies had returned to retrieve a bag which Carla J. Martin had left there. Even a novice private investigator would have been able to track them down well in advance of the trial. Had these three witnesses been able to testify about Washington's behavior prior to going up to his room, Mike Tyson might very well have been acquitted. On March 25, 1995, the *Associated Press* reported that juror David Vahle, and four other jurors, had "developed doubts about the former boxing champion's guilt. These doubts result in part from their learning about the existence of the three defense witnesses who were not permitted to testify at the trial."

There was another very important fact which should have part of the evidence admitted at the trial. Washington claimed she asked Tyson to use a condom, but he said that he didn't have any. I knew that he did. In fact, MT told me that he had used rubbers with B Angie B and "another girl." This showed that Desiree Washington was capable of inventing facts to support her story.

I could have testified about Desiree Washington's two calls to The Big House the afternoon of July 19, 1991. I could have described how she had been offended Mike Tyson wasn't available to speak with her, and that was the day *before* she reported to authorities that he had sexually-assaulted her. Vince Fuller was aware of that very critical fact. He had learned about it at the first meeting we had with him in his fancy DC office five months before the trial. The limousine driver, Virginia Foster, testified that, when Desiree Washington returned from Mike Tyson's hotel room, she complained about him not escorting her back to the limo: "I can't believe him. I can't believe him," she repeated. "Who does he think he is?" Washington didn't sound like a woman who had just been sexually-attacked but rather like one who had just been disrespected.

If I had been allowed to do my job, instead of being kicked off the flight to Indianapolis, I would have been in Room 606 of the Canterbury Hotel while my boss was having sex with Desiree Washington. I also would have escorted her, not only back to the limo waiting for her, but all the way back to her hotel. My duties included making women feel special after having sex with him. He didn't deserve an "A" for being a gentleman, but Mike Tyson was not a rapist. For unknown reasons Vince Fuller and his high-priced legal team had no interest in sitting down with me to learn what I knew which would have been extremely helpful to his defense. That didn't make any sense at all.

One survey taken by an Indianapolis television station revealed that 60% disagreed with the guilty verdict. On April 9, 1994, *The Miami Herald* reported the Indiana Court of Appeals had ruled that a judge needed to review claims

Desiree Washington "had falsely accused" a high school classmate, Wayne Walker, of rape. Walker's mother and one of his football teammates had submitted affidavits confirming that false accusation. Before Mike Tyson's trial, Washington announced to the world that she didn't bring charges against him "to take his career away." Instead, she did it because Tyson "needed help." There were rumors that Washington had been offered $750,000 to drop the charges, but she had refused to take any money. However, once Mike Tyson was convicted, which established his civil liability to her as a matter of law, Desiree Washington soon filed a lawsuit for an unspecified amount of damages.

***

After Mike Tyson was found guilty, many months went by before I was asked to get back into the business of working for a professional fighter. Gladys Rosa, the Don King employee who handled Hispanic boxers, reached out to me. She asked for my assistance to set up a match between one of my childhood friends, Hector "Macho" Camacho, and Julio Cesar Chavez, a Mexican fighter promoted by Don King Productions. At the time I didn't know that Camacho's contract with his promoters, the Duvas, was coming up for renewal. I told Gladys that I would think about it and get back to her. Camacho was staying with his mother in the same roach-infested housing project, Thomas Jefferson Houses, on East 115th Street in Spanish Harlem, where my Mother lived. Two months went by before Camacho agreed to the meeting Gladys Rosa had requested. Macho hired me at $1,000 per day to accompany him and Rosa to South Florida to discuss arrangements for the Julio Cesar Chavez match. We boarded a flight to the West Palm Beach airport.

Our destination was Don King's estate in an exclusive Delray Beach community called Foxe Chase. King had purchased that property for a million dollars right around the time of Mike Tyson's rape trial. He also had relocated Don King Productions to South Florida in nearby Deerfield Beach.

That day Macho Camacho was "jonesing," meaning that he needed to do some coke really bad. Unfortunately, my friend had been having problems with cocaine since his early teens. Camacho believed in *santeria* which combined Catholicism with practices African slaves brought to the New World. Camacho thought that he was protected by a spirit named "Titan" who shared his own spirit. Titan took him to the dark side but also cared for him and saved him from harm. To satisfy Titan, Camacho would "feed" him by ingesting cocaine. During the flight to Florida, I learned that Gladys Rosa had promised Camacho some coke. And it was easy to see that he was desperate to get some.

Don King's driver, Isadore Bolton, picked us up at the airport. Soon we were pulling into the driveway of an enormous white-marble residence next to a beautiful lake located at the rear of the property. There was a big pier, and a glittering speedboat was tied up to it. Bolton ushered us inside where we were greeted by two huge stone lions on pedestals guarding the foyer. I saw the look of amazement on Camacho's face who wasn't used to this kind of wealth whereas I had been around it just about every day for the past five years. Mike Tyson made more money in one fight than Camacho had earned during his entire career. Bolton went to another room where Don King was sitting with a couple of guys and announced our arrival. After a few minutes, Don King strolled in and greeted Camacho. He glanced over at me, but he did not acknowledge my presence. He then turned to Gladys Rosa.

"Are the contracts signed?"

"No, he didn't sign yet."

At that moment Camacho jumped up. "I ain't signing nothing until I get some blow!"

King motioned to Rosa to follow him. About five minutes later she returned carrying a leather portfolio engraved with the logo of Don King Productions. Rosa sat down at the end of the sofa where Macho Camacho was and opened the portfolio. She took out a folder which had the fight contract, then a sandwich bag containing a white, powdery substance.

In Spanish Gladys Rosa said: "I've got ten grams, but the contract must be signed now. And there will be more after it's signed." She added that Camacho would be receiving $100,000 to fight Chavez, and that he would be training in Cleveland at "Mike Tyson's camp."

At that moment I realized that I had become an unwitting participant in a carefully-planned trap. This trip to South Florida was not about Gladys Rosa promoting a fight between Don King-controlled Julio Cesar Chavez and Hector "Macho" Camacho. Until that moment I had been under the impression that I was going to help Gladys Rosa train Camacho for the Chavez fight. Suddenly, I learned this whole charade was about delivering Camacho to Don King so he could sign him as another exclusive property of Don King Productions instead of renewing his contract with the Duvas. Now there no longer was a need for either me or Gladys Rosa to stay involved. That day Camacho agreed to all terms Don King proposed to him just so he could get some blow in his nose as soon as possible.

As we started to leave, Camacho reminded King not to forget about the $100,000 he had promised him. "And the rest of my *perico*," he added. The Spanish word *perico* means parakeet, but it also is slang for cocaine because you just might start talking like one when you did some blow. Camacho went off to Cleveland to train with DKP. The work I had anticipated doing for Macho was not going to happen so I returned to Spanish Harlem.

The same strategy that Gladys Rosa had utilized on Camacho she used on other fighters. One was Mexican boxing great Julio Cesar Chavez. After convincing him that she was "an independent Latin boxing consultant," Rosa worked as his business manager and interpreter. In fact, Gladys Rosa had negotiated various deals for fighters so that Don King would have the upper hand. She didn't hesitate to use cocaine to entice Chavez into the Don King Productions stable. Sadly, Julio Cesar Chavez developed a very bad drug habit. There came a time when he needed professional help. He checked into a rehabilitation facility in Mexico to try and rid himself of this disease. However, the very same day Julio Cesar Chavez was released from it, Gladys Rosa was waiting at the door with fight contracts and more cocaine.

***

In the fall of 1993, I went to Las Vegas to look up an old girlfriend who was working in guest relations at the Golden Nugget. What I originally had planned to be a brief encounter with Heather turned into a six-month stay with her. During that time, she let me use her house, car, beeper, and employee meal tickets good at all the hotels. One night I was having dinner alone at the Showboat when an elderly black gentleman approached me. He was sitting at a nearby table with his family. He told me that he had worked in VIP housekeeping at the Hilton Hotel where Don King had maintained a penthouse suite even though King was living at The Mirage. Don King and John Horne used to meet alone for hours in that penthouse suite. Back then I had thought that it was very weird King and Horne would be together at that other hotel for such long periods of time. This former Hilton employee had recognized me because he had seen me constantly at Mike Tyson's side while he was preparing for the two Razor Ruddock fights.

The older gentleman was concerned about what had happened to Mike Tyson. He found it strange that Tyson had been found guilty of rape and sent to prison. He then related a very bizarre story. One day during the spring of 1991, he was cleaning the Don King penthouse suite when he noticed a large number of files in the master bedroom. Thinking they contained fight photos, he sat on the bed and started looking through them. However, instead of finding what he expected, it turned out that these files contained information, including crime-scene photos, about rape cases. Somebody had been "studying up" on this subject. He remembered one of the rape cases related to somebody named Alexander Pantages. I would learn later that Pantages was a Greek immigrant who owned the second-largest movie theater chain in California. In 1929, Pantages was convicted of the rape of a young girl, Eunice Pringle, and was sentenced to fifty years in prison. After winning his appeal, Pantages was granted a new trial and, two years later, he was found not guilty. Stories began surfacing Eunice Pringle had given a death-bed confession that Joseph P. Kennedy had masterminded a frame-up of Pantages after he had rejected Kennedy's offers to buy his chain of movie theaters.

In the summer of 1994, Ted Watley and Murad Muhammad called me at my Mother's apartment. Watley had been a contract negotiator for Don King Productions where he developed a reputation of getting even the most resistant fighters to sign up. Muhammad had been Razor Ruddock's promoter. They had been following my efforts to clear Mike Tyson's name. Watley told me that Don King had bragged to him: "Tyson had to be taught a lesson." The fact that Ted Watley and Murad Muhammad called me to demonstrate their support gave me even more courage to carry on the struggle to get the truth out about what really happened to Mike Tyson.

***

On November 1, 1994, I flew into Miami after I got a call from Macho Camacho. He wanted to discuss the future of his boxing career. Macho had been a three-time welterweight champion and believed he could win the title again by beating Pernell Whitaker. Macho said that he was having "a small problem" with Don King, and he needed to talk to me in person. After I arrived in Miami, I met up with Elanora, a lady from Italy who was visiting South Florida. I had provided her bodyguard services in the past. She invited me to have dinner with her in Coconut Grove.

While we were at the restaurant, my beeper went off. It was Camacho's trainer who said that Macho would arrive in Miami Beach around midnight, and that I could expect a beep from him at that time. Camacho had been under house arrest at his residence in Clewiston, Florida, part of the terms of conditional release after his conviction for battery on a police officer at the Miami International Airport. The officer had been watching Camacho on a surveillance camera and saw him in possession of drugs. Camacho had an additional problem stemming from that case. He had been ordered to pay substantial restitution.

Around 11 p.m. I took Elanora back to the Park Central Hotel on Ocean Drive in Miami Beach where we shared a glass of wine in the lobby. At 11:20 p.m. Macho paged me and wanted to know my location. A few minutes later Camacho showed up at the hotel with two guys I didn't recognize who looked wired and paranoid.

"We gotta talk," Camacho said.

I told him I had a client with me and couldn't leave her. He insisted this was "business," and we needed to be alone. After saying my goodbyes to Elanora, I left with Camacho for the Clevelander Hotel. Macho was driving a Cadillac rental equipped with a mobile phone. He made several calls, but I still didn't have a clue what this was all about. At the Clevelander Hotel, Camacho went into a rap about the "old days" as he drank one screwdriver after another like they were going out of style. He was acting childish and obnoxious, including grabbing every girl in sight by the ass. And he was looking very foolish with powder on his nose while he continued to get extremely drunk. I wasn't enjoying this at all.

"I left a bag in the car, Rudy," Camacho said.

"There's a lot of jewelry in there. Go get it. It's on the floor underneath the driver's seat."

Camacho tossed me the keys then turned around to order another screwdriver. I exited the hotel feeling very cold and uncomfortable, and then something clicked inside me. There was a real possibility my childhood friend was setting me up. I could have stopped right there and turned around, but I needed to put this friendship to the ultimate test: whether Hector Camacho was capable of doing me harm. Just like he had said, there was a small leather clutch under the driver's seat. When I returned to the bar, Macho was out of his chair, dancing and wiggling wildly. I handed him the clutch.

"You're my bodyguard. It's important you hold on to it," he said, giving me a look which made my skin crawl. "I gotta go to the can," he added.

Before he entered the men's room, Camacho looked back at me with that same weird look that had scared the shit out of me. I knew right then I had to ditch that bag. I flung the clutch into a little storage room and headed for the bathroom to confront Camacho. At that moment a wave of police officers spread across the bar moving directly for me. As they surrounded me I told the officers that I hadn't done anything wrong, that I was there protecting three-time boxing champion Macho Camacho. One of the cops told me there was a report out that someone fitting my description was impersonating a police officer and robbing pedestrians at gunpoint. I assured the officers that they had my full cooperation and wasn't armed. I produced identification showing I was a licensed bodyguard in New York, California, and Nevada. While I was being frisked, I noticed Camacho still hadn't returned from the bathroom. Finally, the officers went looking for him.

Among my personal effects the police had found a badge with the Police Benevolent Association logo. One of my friends from the Florida Highway Patrol had given me that badge. However, this was a problem for one of the officers who didn't like the fact I was carrying around a "Florida badge." He arrested me for "impersonating a police officer" and escorted me out of the hotel. My name was run through the computer, and my record came back clean as a whistle. While I was sitting in the back seat of a police cruiser, Camacho walked out of the hotel. Looking very confident, he approached the cruiser and tapped on the window next to me.

"You should never fuck with Don King!" Camacho said loudly. "Now you're going to jail!"

I still didn't understand what was going on. "Stop fooling around," I told him. "Chill out."

I noticed Camacho's gaze moving toward the front of the police cruiser. All my personal effects taken during the frisk had been spread across the hood. When he didn't see the leather clutch there, Camacho turned back to me with a shocked expression. At that moment he realized his mission had failed. Camacho had given me the punch line before telling me the joke. With that look still written on his face, he disappeared into the darkness. The Dade State Attorney agreed to drop the case against me in exchange for my promise not to take legal action against the City of Miami Beach. The friendship that I had with Hector "Macho" Camacho, which had spanned decades, died that night.

***

There came a time when Patricia J. Gifford, the judge who presided over Mike Tyson's rape trial, offered him the opportunity for early release from his prison term. After serving two years and two months of his six-year sentence, Tyson appeared before Judge Gifford. Camille Ewald, who was eighty-nine by then, testified on his behalf. There were other witnesses who let the Judge know that Tyson had been studying and trying to make himself a better person. Mike Tyson told the Judge that his fame and fortune had come too easily, "like it all just dropped from the sky," and that he was "sorry" for the "situation" and "any pain" caused to Desiree Washington and her family. But Mike Tyson refused to admit that he had raped Desiree Washington. Judge Gifford noted that Tyson had failed his exam for a general-equivalency high school diploma. She added that anyone who had "normal intelligence" and didn't have "a learning disability" should have been able to pass that test if he had worked at it. She also said Tyson's statements about "just being sorry" didn't cut it. With these two things in mind, Judge Gifford denied Mike Tyson's request for early release.

Ferdie Pacheco, the well-known "fight doctor," published an article in *Boxing Illustrated* entitled "Tyson's Moral Choice." To become a free man and start earning millions of dollars again, all Tyson had to do was agree to the label "Mike Tyson, the Rapist" as he stood before Judge Patricia J. Gifford. Pacheco praised Mike Tyson for his refusal to accept that label. He "became an admirable man in my eyes," Ferdie Pacheco wrote. "If he never wins another boxing match, he will go down as 'Mike Tyson, Champion'...I am proud of Mike Tyson. Tyson's choice is an achievement which exceeds anything he has done before. So, let the wise guys laugh in their beers. I lift my glass to 'Mike Tyson, The Man.'"

On May 18, 1992, *Sports Illustrated* reported that Bill Cayton had filed suit against Don King, alleging that he skimmed millions from Tyson fight purses. In a deposition in that case, Mohammed Khan, Tyson's former accountant, testified that Tyson had only a few million dollars in assets, some real estate, a few cars, and an annuity. Joseph Maffia, the former Don King Productions comptroller, provided an affidavit in which he stated that much of Tyson's money went to Don King and his family. He also said that King had skimmed millions off Tyson fight purses before Tyson collected his 66.6% share and King his 33.3% promoter's fee. King responded that Joseph Maffia's testimony was filled with lies, fabrications, and half-truths. "I have never improperly taken anything from Mike," Don King fired back, "and every expense was at his direction or approval."

The day the guilty verdict in my boss's rape trial was handed down, I believed it was the end. All I wanted to do was distance myself from everything that had been going on, erasing it from my memory, just as I had done with the pocket computer delivered into the hands of John Horne. But six-thousand miles far away from home, as I lay on a beach in Rio de Janeiro, I could not put behind me what had happened. Mike Tyson had given me the opportunity of a lifetime and made me part of his "inner ring." He had continued to trust and support me over the years no matter how much others had tried to sabotage our relationship. Back in my Mother's apartment in New York, my Tyson jackets were hanging in a closet, representing the real tradition behind this world champion heavyweight fighter. I had witnessed how so many people had cared for Mike Tyson through the years, and how he had cared for them, before others were able to take control over every part of his life. And I had witnessed the enormous deceit and betrayal and fraud committed upon Mike Tyson.

There had been so much light in the first few years and so much darkness during the last two. Once I made the drive up to The White House to check up on Camille Ewald who by then had turned ninety-years-old. Before I went there, I stopped by Junior's in Brooklyn to pick up some of her favorite cheesecake. When I arrived at The White House that night, I noticed that Camille had lit a number of candles in the dining room. It turned out that she didn't have enough money to pay her electric bill.

All the letters I sent to Mike Tyson at the Plainfield, Indiana prison were returned to me undelivered, stamped "unauthorized mail." I called the prison to find out why MT couldn't receive my mail. I was told that I would have to go through the attorneys for Don King Productions. After my boss was sent to prison, I checked around about the status of his large inventory of luxury cars. I found out that most of them had been auctioned off, many below commercial value, with others receiving the proceeds.

As the Brazilian sun bathed me in its light and warmth, I could not stop thinking about Mike Tyson sitting alone in a cold and dark prison cell. He never should have ended up there. And then I knew exactly what I had to do. Mike Tyson never fired me and, as far as I was concerned, I still worked for him. The story of Mike Tyson's life did not have to end in February of 1992 when an Indianapolis jury found him guilty of rape. Instead, another story could begin filled with light and truth. I still had the Wizard disc and copies of papers made with my hand-held Panasonic. They helped document the enormous fraud, deceit, and betrayal visited upon my boss. And they would help me tell the story about what *really* happened to Mike Tyson.

POSTSCRIPT

On June 22, 1992, just a few months after Mike Tyson was found guilty of rape in Indianapolis, Desiree Washington filed a lawsuit against him for an unspecified amount of damages. Deval L. Patrick, her Boston attorney, said: "Ms. Washington decided to bring this case only after much soul-searching." Patrick later became a two-term Governor of Massachusetts. Harvard law professor Alan Dershowitz, who was handling Tyson's appeal, observed this case demonstrated Washington's greed and ambition. Dershowitz said: "We were just waiting for her true colors to show through. I predicted right from the beginning that this is a pot-at-the-end-of-the-rainbow suit." While Tyson still was serving his sentence, the case was put on hold. On March 25, 1995, Mike Tyson was released from prison. However, less than three months later, Desiree Washington suddenly dropped her lawsuit. It is unknown what amount of money, if any, she received in that case.

On March 5, 1998, Tyson filed suit against Don King in federal court in Manhattan. The next day *The New York Times* reported that he was "alleging a brazen and vast decade-long pattern of financial fraud and abuse that robbed the troubled former heavyweight boxing champion of tens of millions of dollars." Tyson was seeking "at least $100 million in damages and lost earnings," accusing King of "duping [him] into signing a contract while the boxer was still in prison...assigning Tyson a pair of fake managers who, acting on King's behalf, siphoned off huge chunks of the fighter's purses, and using millions of dollars that should have gone to Tyson to pay King's wife and children exorbitant and bogus consulting fees."

On March 10, 1998, just days after he filed suit against Don King in New York, Mike Tyson filed a lawsuit against John Horne and Rory Holloway in Los Angeles Superior Court. In that case, Tyson alleged he lost millions of dollars because Horne and Holloway convinced him, while he was still in prison, to sign a contract with Don King. Tyson didn't know they would receive 20 percent of his purses and King another 30 percent. Tyson's lawyers claimed Horne and Holloway were "puppets" who never performed any serious management services and existed as "little more than window dressing for King."

Mike Tyson listed Rudy Gonzalez as a witness in the cases he filed against King, Horne, and Holloway. On January 29, 1999, a group of high-powered defense attorneys in the two cases arrived in Miami to take Rudy's video deposition which ended up lasting the entire day. His testimony was crucial to support Tyson's claims in those lawsuits. I was present to assist Rudy if he needed my legal help. He never did. Rudy totally disarmed those lawyers, providing critical facts Tyson needed to prove his claims. Sadly, however, Mike Tyson never had his day in court. On August 1, 2003, he filed petitions for Chapter 11 protection in the United States Bankruptcy Court in Manhattan. Tyson's debts totaled more than $38 million, including $13.4 million he owed to the Internal Revenue Service. The two cases pending against Don King, John Horne, and Rory

Holloway then were deemed Mike Tyson "assets," and the bankruptcy trustee took control over them. On June 24, 2004, the bankruptcy court approved a settlement in the $100 million case against Don King in exchange for his payment of only $14 million. Mike Tyson never saw a penny of that settlement because those funds were destined to pay down his enormous debts.

In 2004, Rory Holloway and John Horne filed suit against Don King, and that case ended up in federal court in Manhattan. Holloway and Horne alleged that Don King breached an agreement to pay them ten percent of all of his earnings from exploiting Tyson fights. However, they had a fundamental problem. Holloway and Horne never had their agreement with King reduced to writing. The oral agreement was legally impossible to enforce. Don King filed a motion to dismiss. The federal judge granted the motion and entered final judgment in favor of King.

At the time of release of this edition of *The Inner Ring*, Mike Tyson resides in the Seven Hills subsection of Henderson, Nevada about seven miles from the Las Vegas Strip. Tyson has had three marriages, first to Robin Givens in 1988, a union which lasted only one year. In 1997, he married Monica Turner, a pediatric physician, and their marriage ended in divorce in 2003. In 2009, Tyson married longtime girlfriend Lakiha "Kiki" Spicer. He has fathered seven children. One of his daughters, Exodus, died in a tragic accident when she was four-years-old.

On November 20, 2012, Hector "Macho" Camacho was shot in the face in a friend's car in Bayamon, Puerto Rico. His friend, Adrian Mojica Moreno, was shot dead on the spot. Two men fled the scene in a sport utility vehicle.

Nine bags of cocaine were found in Moreno's pockets and a tenth one open in the car. Camacho was taken off life support four days later. He was fifty-years-old. Rudy was a pallbearer at his funeral in New York. The service was held at St. Cecilia in East Harlem, the church Camacho attended as a young boy. A former pastor remembered him from the seventies, telling the mourners that Camacho "could lift us up, and he could break our hearts. He could inspire us and at times he could disappoint us." Three years earlier, Camacho reached out to Rudy to try and reestablish their lifelong friendship, confessing to him the sin he had committed on behalf of Don King.

Mike Tyson earned more than $400 million during his boxing career, but his current net worth is estimated to be only $3 million. A few years ago, Kevin Rooney, Mike Tyson's lead trainer with the original "Team Tyson," stated: "Mike could have been 100-0 and made a billion dollars if he had stayed with me." Why *didn't* Mike Tyson stay with Kevin Rooney and the original "Team Tyson"? The real answer to that question lies within *The Inner Ring*.

Martin Alan Feigenbaum
Surfside, Florida
December, 2017

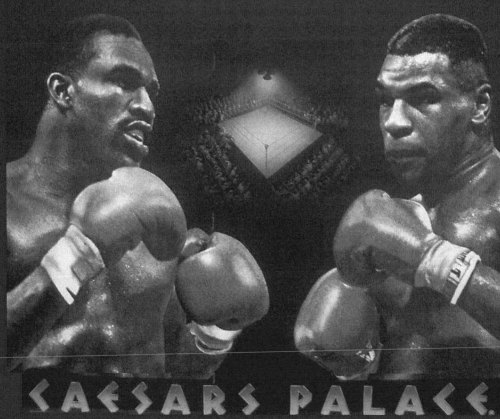

WORLD
HEAVYWEIGHT CHAMPIONSHIP
HOLYFIELD
TYSON
NOVEMBER 8, 1991

CAESARS PALACE

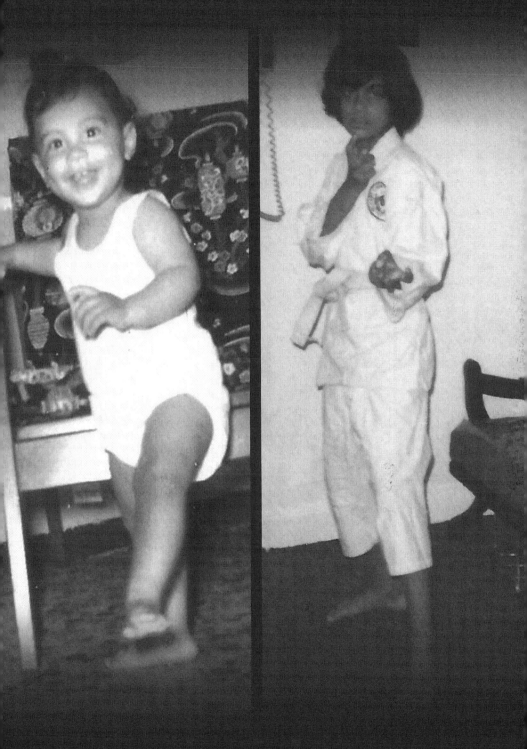

Rudy at one already learning how to kick.

Rudy at the age of 10 in his early aikido martial arts training at his home in Spanish Harlem.

Rudy Gonzalez TEAM TYSON gear

During the more than five years I worked for Mike Tyson, I was officially off-duty five times. My boss didn't give me a lot of nights off, but when he did, he told me to take the jet. Here Rudy is having dinner with his Italian girlfriend Gina DelRosso.

The Genesis Coach built for Tyson

Rudy Gonzalez designed this Genesis Coach with the assistance of Mattel Toys. This $3.5 million armored beauty was Priority One for Mike Tyson, his "escape vehicle" from Don King. But King had other plans for Tyson.

This Genesis Coach was a heavily armored two-bedroom penthouse on wheels with a one-car garage accessible using a retractor at the rear bumper.

Luxury accommodations included gold fixtures, a rotating "sky bed," two safes, and a bodyguard command center with 360-degree surveillance cameras and tear-gas defense for crowd control.

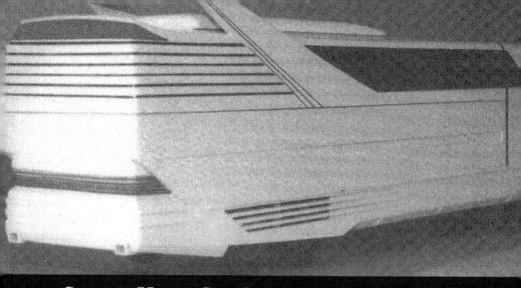

Genesis Motor Coach
Model by Mattel Toys; Design by Rudy Gonzalez.

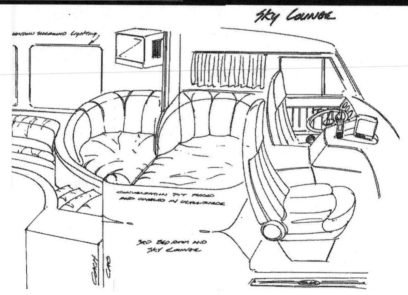

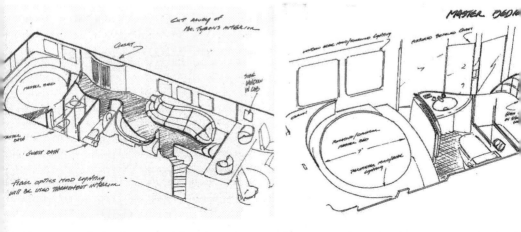

Jim Jacobs, Mike Tyson, and Bill Cayton. A very rare and beautiful photo of the beginning of Team Tyson circa 1985.

Rooney, Lott, Tyson, Baranski

Seen here: Kevin Rooney, Tyson, Matt Baranski, and Steve Lott. With this highly-skilled and fiercely devoted team, Cus D'Amato built the greatest heavyweight fighter of all time. But Don King later would send Mike Tyson down a dark path which eventually would destroy him. D'Amato's words still echo in my heart: "Don't do what the champion wants you to do. You do what's right for the champion." Mike Tyson gave me the opportunity of a lifetime for which I always shall be eternally grateful.

Mike Tyson in luxury hotel suite in Europe.

Rory Holloway and John Horne

Harry Winston 10kt Platinum Champion Ring

Tyson and Naomi Campbell strolling on boardwalk in Atlantic City near his penthouse

Tyson and girlfriend Naomi Campbell and Don King making sure she doesn't get too close.

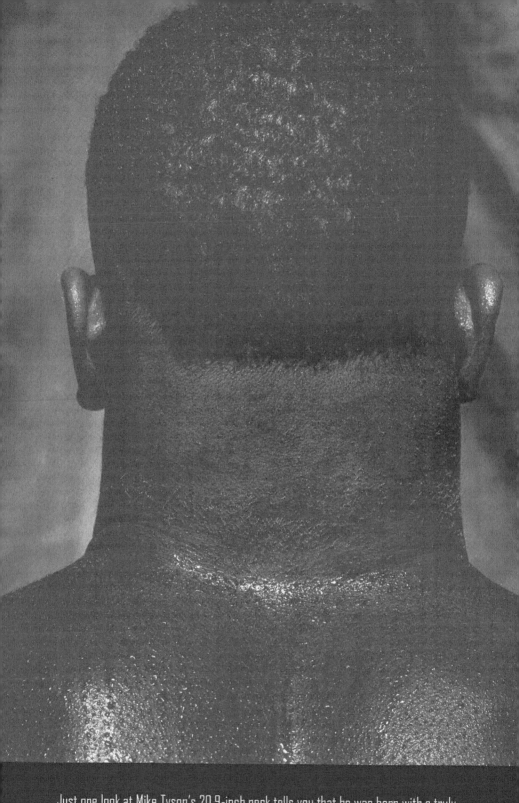

Just one look at Mike Tyson's 20.9-inch neck tells you that he was born with a truly extraordinary physique. He performed 500 neck rolls per workout to get it so muscular.

PAYROLL

MIKE TYSON PRODUCTIONS 12-58
TRAINING ACCOUNT NO. 2
32 E. 69TH ST.
NEW YORK CITY, NY 10021

1830

94-15/1212

1/16 _____ 19 91

PAY RUDY GONZALEZ _____ $ 2,463.93

THOUSAND FOUR HUNDRED SIXTY-THREE AND 93/100 _____ Dollars

SECURITY
PACIFIC BANK
NEVADA

NEVADA FINANCIAL CTR. OFFICE 16
P.O. BOX 18435
LAS VEGAS, NEVADA 89114

REIMBURSEMENT OF EXPENSES

"XXXXXXX" "XXXXXXXXX" "XXXXXXXXXX

MIKE TYSON

PAY ....

FIRST CHICAGO
THE FIRST NATIONAL BANK

MIKE TYSON

FIRST CHICAGO
THE FIRST NATIONAL BANK OF CHICAGO
CHICAGO, ILLINOIS 60670

2-1/710   004447
4447

CHECK
NUMBER

PAY ********* TWO THOUSAND FIVE HUNDRED EIGHTY ONE ********** 67/100 Dollars

Rudy Gonzalez

TO THE
ORDER
OF Rudy Gonzalez
RUDOLPH GONZALEZ
218 EAST 104th STREET
NEW YORK, NY 100

Nov 12 91   DATE   **$2.581.67*   AMOUNT

AUTHORIZED SIGNATURE

"XXXXXXX" ":0 XXXXXXXXX: 6XX XXXXX"

Samples of Rudy's only request was that Mike Tyson sign his payrole check and not John or Rory

EVIDENCE

8-16-94

For Whom it may Concern,
    This is to Confirm that as of this
day Boxer Micheal G. Tyson has
Contracted in good faith the services
of John K. Horne and Rory Holloway
to be his Co-Managers of his Boxing
and Personal Career. They have my
complete trust and faith to represent
my best interest with anyone concerning
my boxing interest. They have the
absolute right to negotiate on my
behalf. ~~~~~ No deal or commitment
on my behalf will be ~~~~~ Complete
without ~~~ John K. Horne and Rory
Holloway Consent and agreement.
    All my ring negotiations with
all Promoters and Media Companys must
be handled by only JKH and R.H. This
is a temporary Contract with a formal
and more detailed one to Come.

Sandra K. Nelson
SANDRA K. NELSON
Hendricks County
Commission Expires
12-7-95

Mike Tyson
8/16/94

Below Mike Tyson real signature

[signature in box]

One of the most outrageous pieces of evidence in the Mike Tyson tragedy is this handwritten "contract" Horne
and Holloway created to allegedly "sign" Tyson while he still was in prison. However, compare the fake Tyson
signature affixed to this "contract" to Tyson's genuine signature.

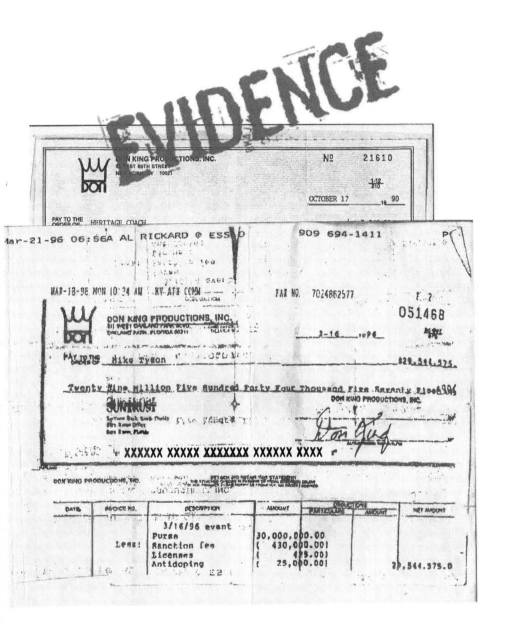

Don King and his two disciples, John Horne and Rory Holloway, pocketed 80% of Mike Tyson's earnings and also charged him for inflated expenses.

Tyson's "peek-a-boo" stance with constant head movement. Bobbing and weaving made him more difficult to hit and enhanced the "peek-a-boo's" effectiveness.

"A boy comes to me with a spark and interest. I feed the spark, and it becomes a flame. I feed the flame, and it becomes a fire. I feed the fire, and it becomes a roaring blaze."

(January 17, 1908 – November 4, 1985)   Cus D'Amato

Mike Tyson unified the Heavyweight Division, and Don King made sure he didn't slip away, not

even for an interview, unless King's disciple, John Horne, shadowed Tyson's every move.

BOUGHT FROM

DATE 5/2/19 91

SOLD TO DON KING PRODUCTIONS
32 EAST 69TH STREET
New York, N.Y. 1002

OCC.		AGE	HEIGHT	.	WEIGHT	TIME	PERMIT NO.		SHIELD NO.	

QUANTITY		DESCRIPTION	PRICE		TOTAL	
1		POINT BLANK MOD 15				
		SIDE PANEL WHITE 46R			850	
		(TAKEN)				
1		PRINT BLANK MOD 15				
		SIDE PANEL WHITE 46R				
		(BACK ORDER)				
		TO BE SHIPPED				

Paid in full

ck# 001473

TEAM TYSON ~ top row: John Horne, Anthony Pitts, Rudy Gonzalez, Gladys Rosa, Don King, John Goldberg,
bottom row: Mike Tyson, & Rory Holloway

World-renowned leather designer Jeff Hamilton with Mike Tyson.

Through all the years with my boss the only time I saw him happy and in peace is with his pigeons.

PAYMENT OPTION	☐ CHECK/MONEY ORDER $35.15	☐ MASTERCARD ☐ VISA $36.07	CHARGE ACCOUNT #		CARD EXP.

183VZWAT2OF

TYSON*MIKE
RT 45
ORWELL   OH   44076

PLATE CAT. PASSENGER   PLATE NO. 183VZW   EPA NO
PLATE TYPE   TITLE NO. 04028L042   OLD APP. BH7998A
VEH. TYPE 4S YEAR 85 MAKE ROLS WGT.
VIN SCAZN42ANFCX13715   PURCHASE DATE 10/04/89
REG. WILL EXPIRE 06/30/91   RENEWAL WILL EXPIRE 06/30/92
TAX DIST. 0491   DISTRICT NAME ORWELL
COUNTY ASHTABULA   SSN OR TAX I.D. NUMBER

PROOF OF FINANCIAL RESPONSIBILITY

SIGNATURE OF OWNER   JOINT OWNER SIGNATURE 5/21/91   DATE   BMV-4604

X

WARNING: Applicant giving false information is subject to prosecution O.R.C. Section 2921.13. Application must be signed by the owner(s) as named on certificate or title.

T2OF A 183VZW 003515 003607 063091 063092 4S85ROLS RNWL 2

PAYMENT OPTION	☑ CHECK/MONEY ORDER $40.15	☐ MASTERCARD ☐ VISA $41.19	CHARGE ACCOUNT #		CARD EXP.

740XAJAT2WL

TYSON*MIKE
8083 CHUB RD
WINDSOR   OH   44099

PLATE CAT. PASSENGER   PLATE NO. 740XAJ   EPA NO
PLATE TYPE   TITLE NO. 040316344   OLD APP. XV6752
VEH. TYPE 2S YEAR 90 MAKE MERC WGT.
VIN WDBFA66E7LF007928   PURCHASE DATE 06/20/90
REG. WILL EXPIRE 06/30/91   RENEWAL WILL EXPIRE 06/30/92
TAX DIST. 0491   DISTRICT NAME WINDSOR
COUNTY ASHTABULA   SSN OR TAX I.D. NUMBER

PROOF OF FINANCIAL RESPONSIBILITY

SIGNATURE OF OWNER   JOINT OWNER SIGNATURE 5/30/91   DATE   BMV-4604

X

WARNING: Applicant giving false information is subject to prosecution O.R.C. Section 2921.13. Application must be signed by the owner(s) as named on certificate or title.

T2WL A 740XAJ 004015 004119 063091 063092 2S90MERC RNWL

PAYMENT OPTION	☑ CHECK/MONEY ORDER $40.15	☐ MASTERCARD ☐ VISA $41.19	CHARGE ACCOUNT #		CARD EXP.

491XQRAT2WH

TYSON*MICHAEL
8083 CHUB RD
WINDSOR   OH   44099

PLATE CAT. PASSENGER   PLATE NO. 491XQR   EPA NO
PLATE TYPE   TITLE NO. 040332533   OLD APP. XV73100
VEH. TYPE SW YEAR 87 MAKE FOR WGT.
VIN 1FMCA11U5HZA26405   PURCHASE DATE 10/23/90
REG. WILL EXPIRE 06/30/91   RENEWAL WILL EXPIRE 06/30/92
TAX DIST. 0491   DISTRICT NAME WINDSOR
COUNTY ASHTABULA   SSN OR TAX I.D. NUMBER

PROOF OF FINANCIAL RESPONSIBILITY

SIGNATURE OF OWNER   JOINT OWNER SIGNATURE 5/30/91   DATE   BMV-4604

X

WARNING: Applicant giving false information is subject to prosecution O.R.C. Section 2921.13. Application must be signed by the owner(s) as named on certificate or title.

T2WH A 491XQR 004015 004119 063091 063092 SW87FOR RNWL 0

PAYMENT OPTION	☑ CHECK/MONEY ORDER $40.15	☐ MASTERCARD ☐ VISA $41.19	CHARGE ACCOUNT #		CARD EXP.

493XQRAT2WK

TYSON*MICHAEL
8083 CHUB RD
WINDSOR   OH   44099

PLATE CAT. PASSENGER   PLATE NO. 493XQR   EPA NO
PLATE TYPE   TITLE NO. 040332556   OLD APP. XV73102
VEH. TYPE 2S YEAR 89 MAKE PORS WGT.
VIN WPOEB0912KS173064   PURCHASE DATE 10/23/90
REG. WILL EXPIRE 06/30/91   RENEWAL WILL EXPIRE 06/30/92
TAX DIST. 0491   DISTRICT NAME WINDSOR
COUNTY ASHTABULA   SSN OR TAX I.D. NUMBER

PROOF OF FINANCIAL RESPONSIBILITY

SIGNATURE OF OWNER   JOINT OWNER SIGNATURE 5/30/91   DATE   BMV-4604

X

WARNING: Applicant giving false information is subject to prosecution O.R.C. Section 2921.13. Application must be signed by the owner(s) as named on certificate or title.

T2WK A 493XQR 004015 004119 063091 063092 2S89PORS RNWL 2

DETACH HERE	APPLICATION FOR RENEWAL REGISTRATION BY MAIL	MAIL THIS PART

PAYMENT OPTION: ☑ CHECK/MONEY ORDER $40.15 ☐ MASTERCARD $41.15 ☐ VISA CHARGE ACCOUNT # CARD EXP.

492XQRAT2WK

TYSON*MICHAEL
8083 CHUB RD
WINDSOR   OH   44099

PLATE CAT. PASSENGER PLATE NO. 492XQR IPA NO
PLATE TYPE TITLE NO. 040332534 OLD APP. XV73101
VEH. TYPE 25 YEAR A9 MAKE FERR WGT.
VIN 7FFFC33A4K0082083 PURCHASE DATE 10/23/90
REG. WILL EXPIRE 06/30/91 RENEWAL WILL EXPIRE 06/30/92
TAX DIST. 0491 DISTRICT NAME WINDSOR
COUNTY ASHTABULA SSN OR TAX I.D. NUMBER

PROOF OF FINANCIAL RESPONSIBILITY

SIGNATURE OF OWNER
X _____   JOINT OWNER SIGNATURE 5/30/91 DATE BMV-4604

WARNING: Applicant providing false information is subject to prosecution O.R.C. Section 2921.13. Application must be signed by the owner(s) as named on certificate of title.

T2WK A 492XQR 004015 004119 063091 063092 2SA9FFRR RNWI

Mike Tyson real signature

Some of Mike Tyson's car registrations. Notice the signatures.
Mike Tyson did not sign them. Henrietta King, Don King's
wife signed them.

Tyson would purchase a car, and then Don King would register the car to the
Mike Tyson Fan Club, Inc., a corporation Henrietta King and Don King's daughter,
Debbie King, owned. Henrietta King also was signing Mike Tyson's fight contracts.

Don King gave strict instructions that Mike Tyson was not to sign autographs.
King did not want Tyson's authentic signature to be publicly known.

Mike Tyson's private underground garage at the Ocean Club in Atlantic City, housing of some of his East Coast car collection.

Tyson bought them. Rudy drove them and took care of them.

Tyson owned one of the most outrageous and expensive exotic car collections in the world. Tyson's 500SEL Mercedes-Benz heavily-armored bullet-proof limousine.

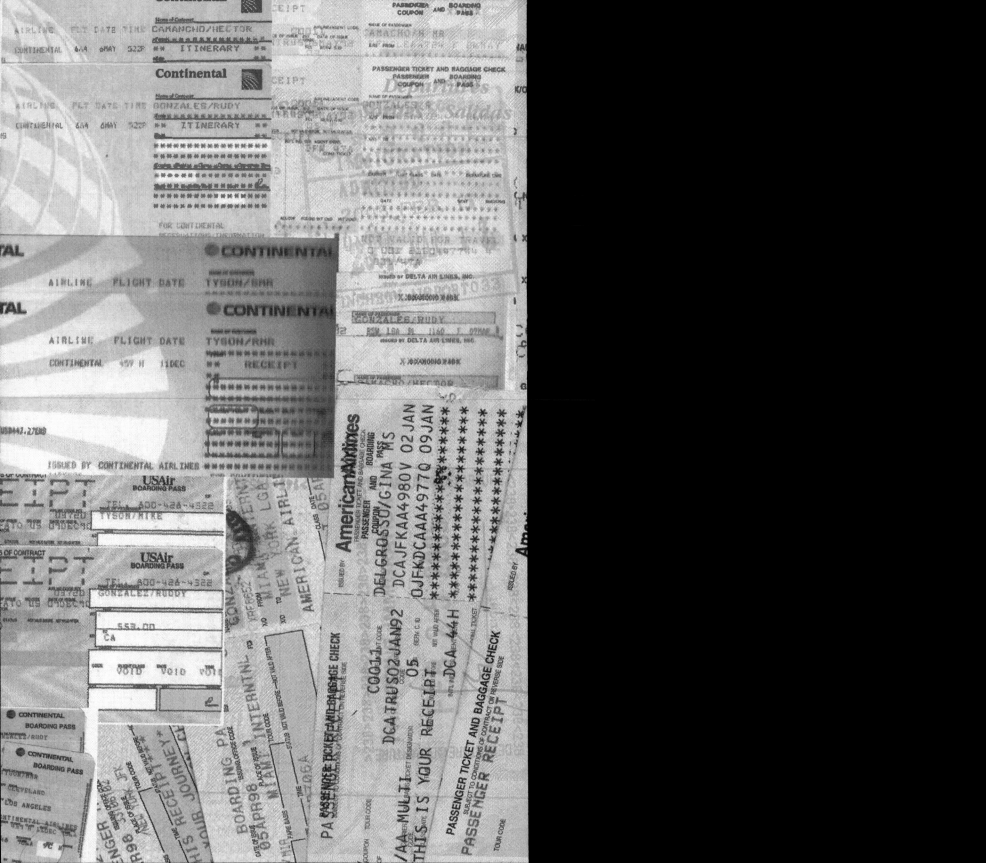

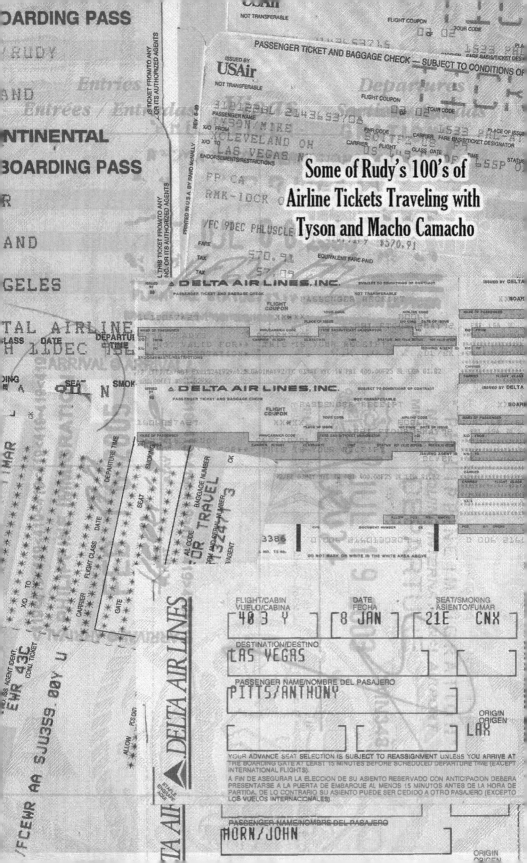

Some of Rudy's 100's of
Airline Tickets Traveling with
Tyson and Macho Camacho

10-Time World Champion Hector "Macho" Camacho with Don King

Always by his side, Rudy with "Macho" Camacho; Camacho
is wearing his world championship belt under his t-shirt; also shown,
Rudy's Miami girlfriend Ileana Campos.

"Macho, I will carry the pain with me forever, of not being there with you, of not being able to protect you, of not being able to shield you from those bullets. With every glittering reflection of metal, I see your championship belts. Our journeys began together growing up poor in our humble Spanish Harlem neighborhood. As fate would have it, we both entered into the world of professional boxing. You became a world-champion prizefighter, and I became part of "the inner ring" of the greatest heavyweight fighter of all time. One-night years later our paths would cross where you betrayed our years of friendship and trust. You died for me that night, but it would not be forever. So many years of good times do not fade from memory so easily. We renewed our bonds of friendship and trust and had more good years before you left us. Macho, I am holding on to you, and I will never let go."

Rudy Gonzalez

Mike Tyson was the youngest boxer ever to win the WBC, WBA, and IBF heavyweight titles, and the only heavyweight fighter to successfully unify them.

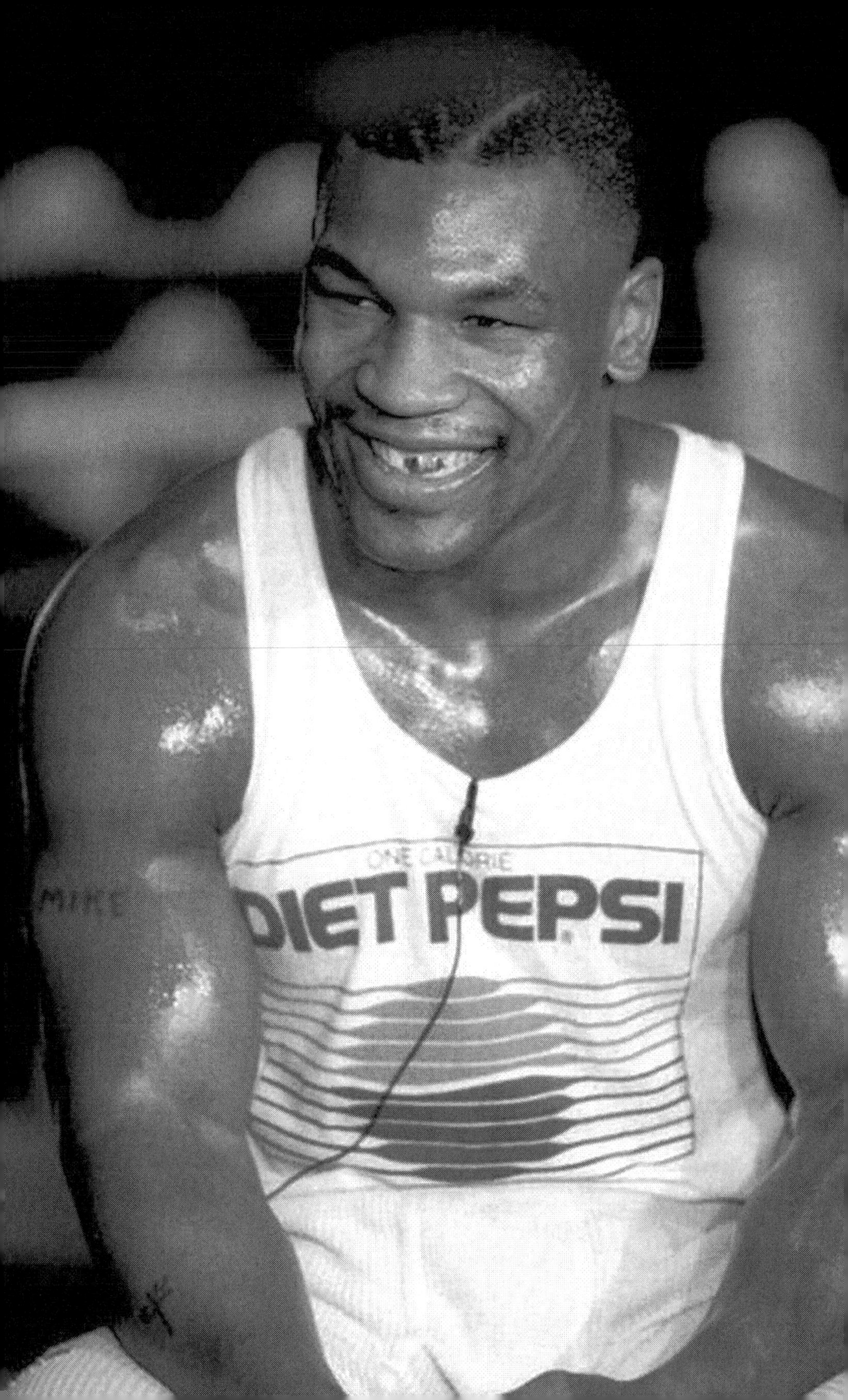
DIET PEPSI

Through all the chaos and madness which overtook Mike Tyson's life, I still was able to see that he possessed a soul filled with great kindness and caring for the weak, vulnerable, and oppressed. Safe passage, my boss, safe passage forever.

The Inner Ring Photo Credits

Dedication to Denise Tyson Anderson - courtesy of Rudy Gonzalez © Rudy Gonzalez

Jim Jacobs, Mike Tyson, and Bill Cayton - courtesy of Steve Lott
© Steve Lott/Boxing Hall of Fame Las Vegas

Rooney, Lott, Tyson, Baranski - courtesy of Steve Lott
© Steve Lott/Boxing Hall of Fame Las Vegas

Mike Tyson with his pigeons - courtesy of Steve Lott
© Steve Lott/Boxing Hall of Fame Las Vegas

Cus D'Amato and his famous quote - courtesy of Steve Lott
© Steve Lott/Boxing Hall of Fame Las Vegas

Tyson/Naomi Campbell on Atlantic City boardwalk
courtesy of Bruce Weber © Bruce Weber

Tyson/Naomi Campbell posing on ground
courtesy of Bruce Weber © Bruce Weber

Tyson 20.9-inch neck - courtesy of Albert Watson © Albert Watson

Hector "Macho" Camacho and Don King - © Getty Images

Don King holding Tyson's arm after Tyson unifies Heavyweight Division - © SI.com

Mike Tyson with WBC, WBA, and IBF belts and Tyson's autograph
courtesy of Rudy Gonzalez © Amazon memorabilia

Don King jacket with quote "on Don King" - courtesy of Timothy A. Clary © Timothy A. Clary

All other photos, graphics, and images - courtesy of Rudy Gonzalez © Rudy Gonzalez

Book cover graphics by Bobby Paulino (Star Shooter Media) and Rudy Gonzalez

Who could have imagined that, what started out as the opportunity of a lifetime for me, would end up as the greatest tragedy in the history of boxing? I witnessed, not only the destruction of the greatest heavyweight fighter to ever step into a ring, but also the destruction of his soul.

Rudy Gonzalez

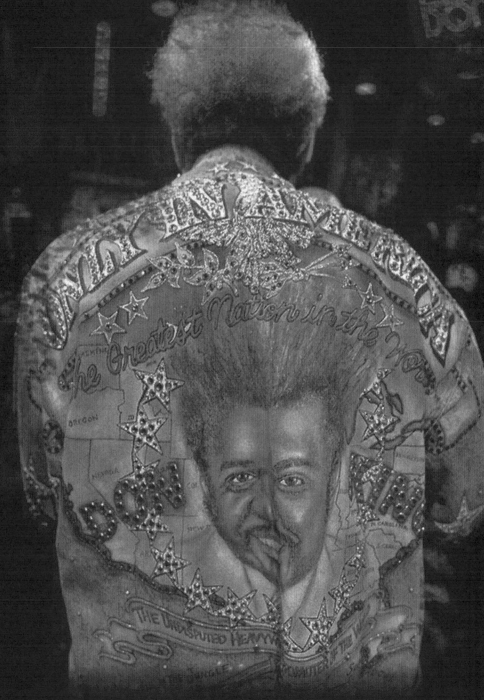

"Only in America, can a black man make all his money in gaming, murder two people, go to prison, and finally become a celebrity and be invited to the White House"

Martin Alan Feigenbaum is an attorney who resides in South Florida.

He holds degrees from Yale University, the Thunderbird School of Global Management, and the University of Miami School of Law. He is the author of Guardians of the Faith, a novel about racism and political correctness, and a prize-winning legal writer in constitutional law.

"Monsters exist, but they are too few in number to be truly dangerous. More dangerous are the common men, the functionaries ready to believe and to act without asking questions."

Primo Levi

Made in the USA
Middletown, DE
13 June 2019